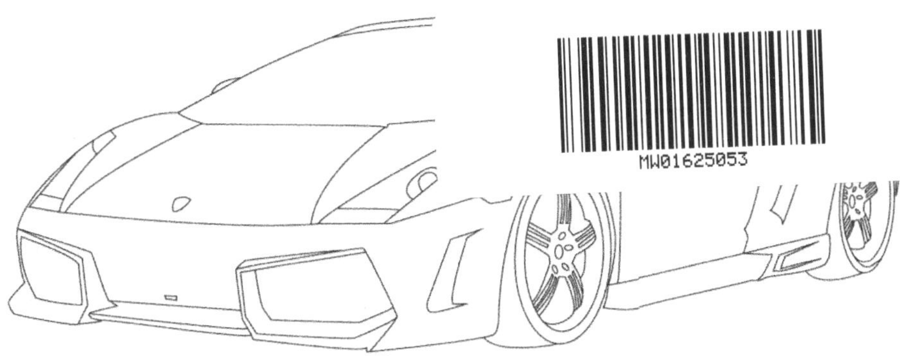

How to Draw Super Cars With Step By Step Illustrations

Master the Art of Drawing 3D Super Cars like Bugatti, Lamborghini, McLaren, Dodge, Ford & Chevrolet

By

Amber Forrest

Published By:
Amber Forrest

Website : www.amberforrest.com

ISBN: 978-81-946896-3-8

McLaren P1

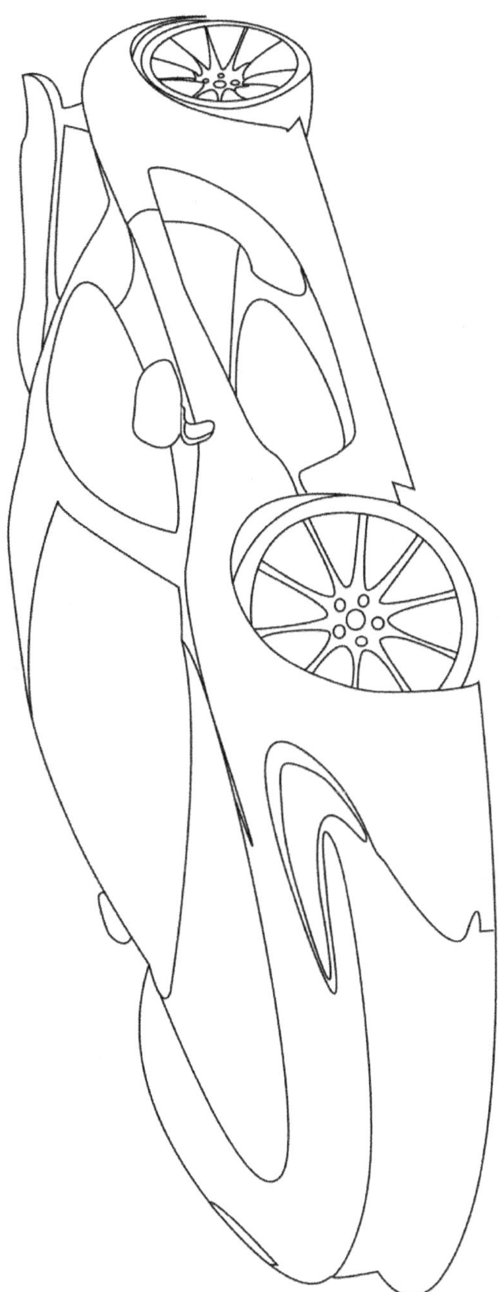

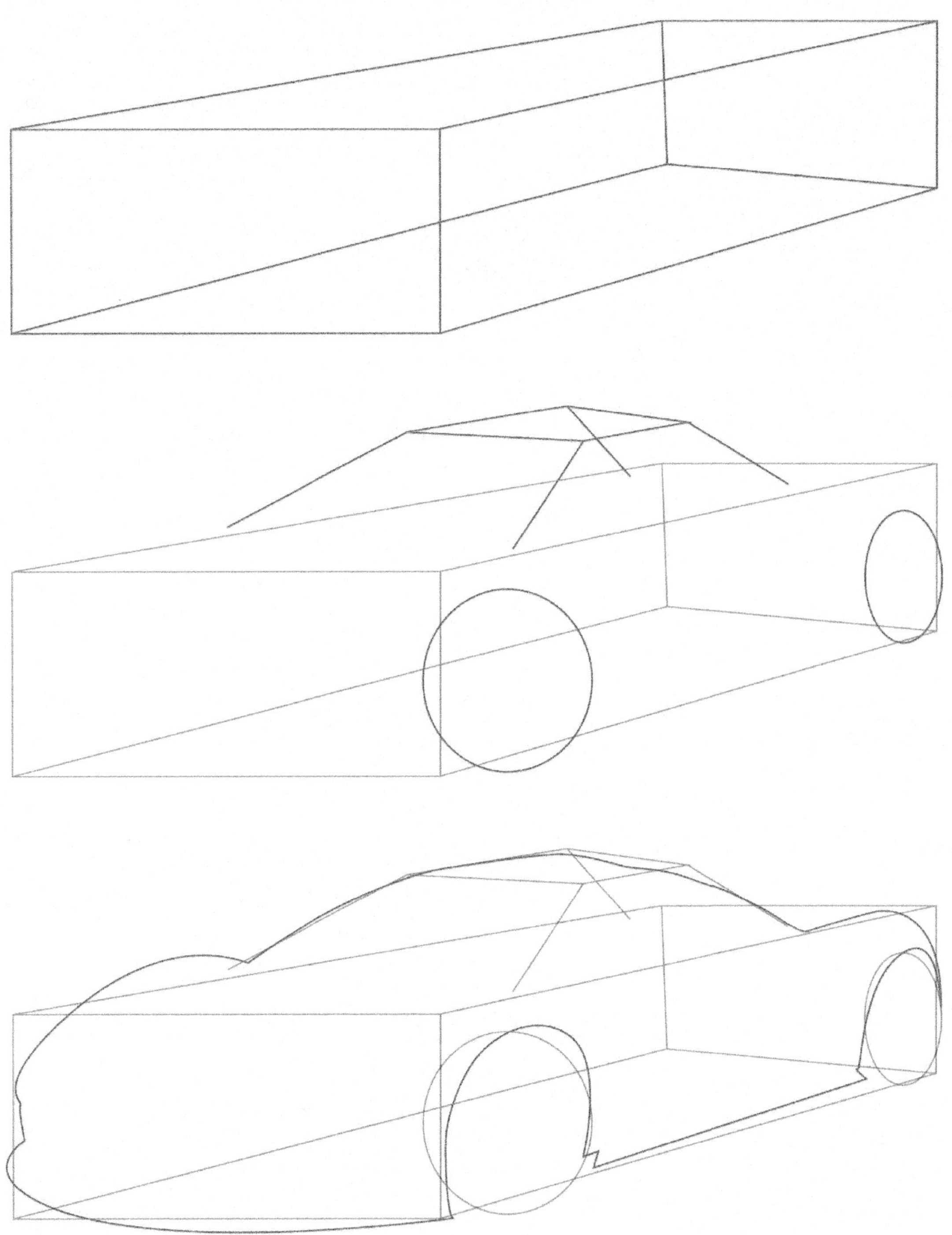

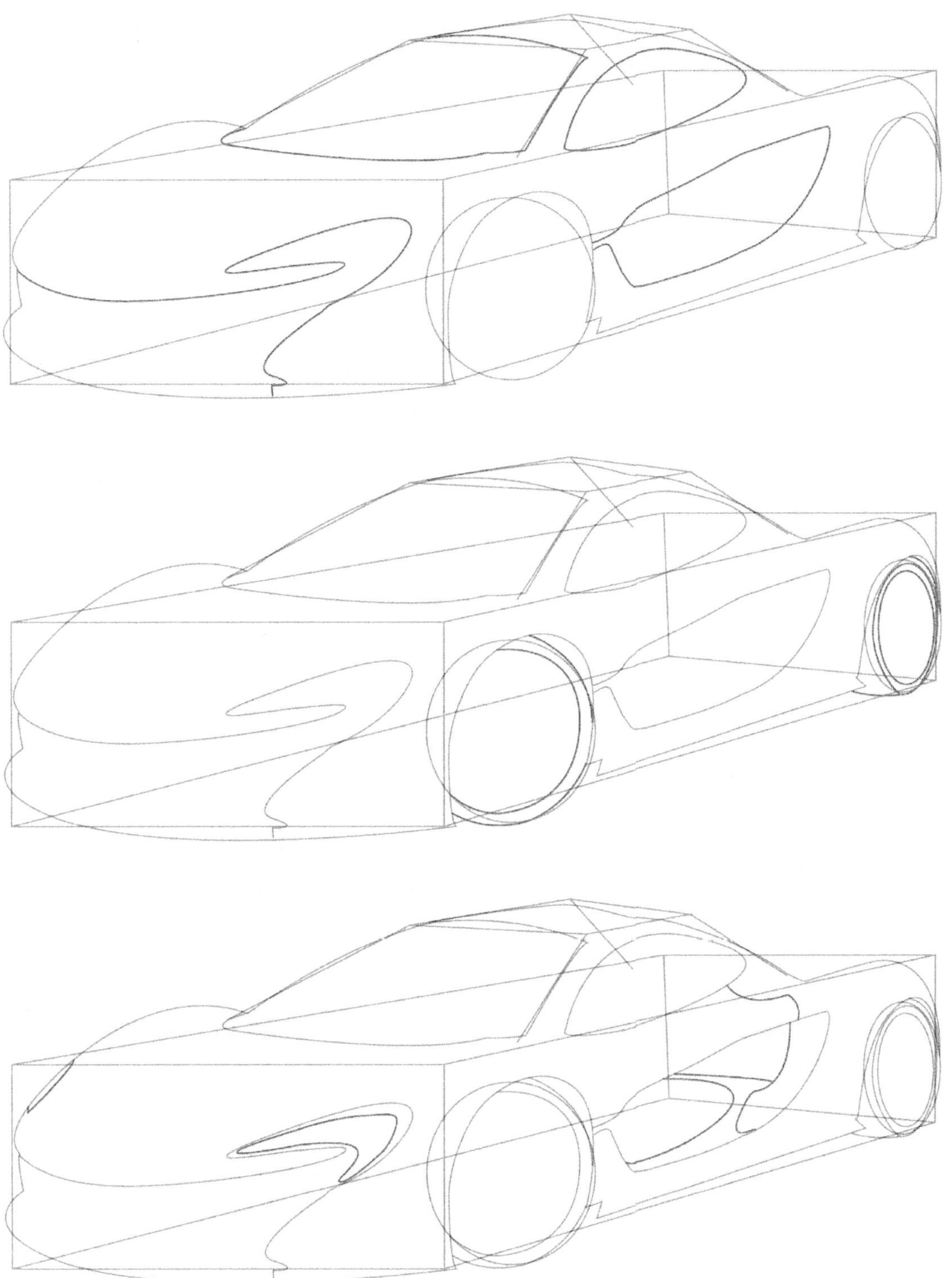

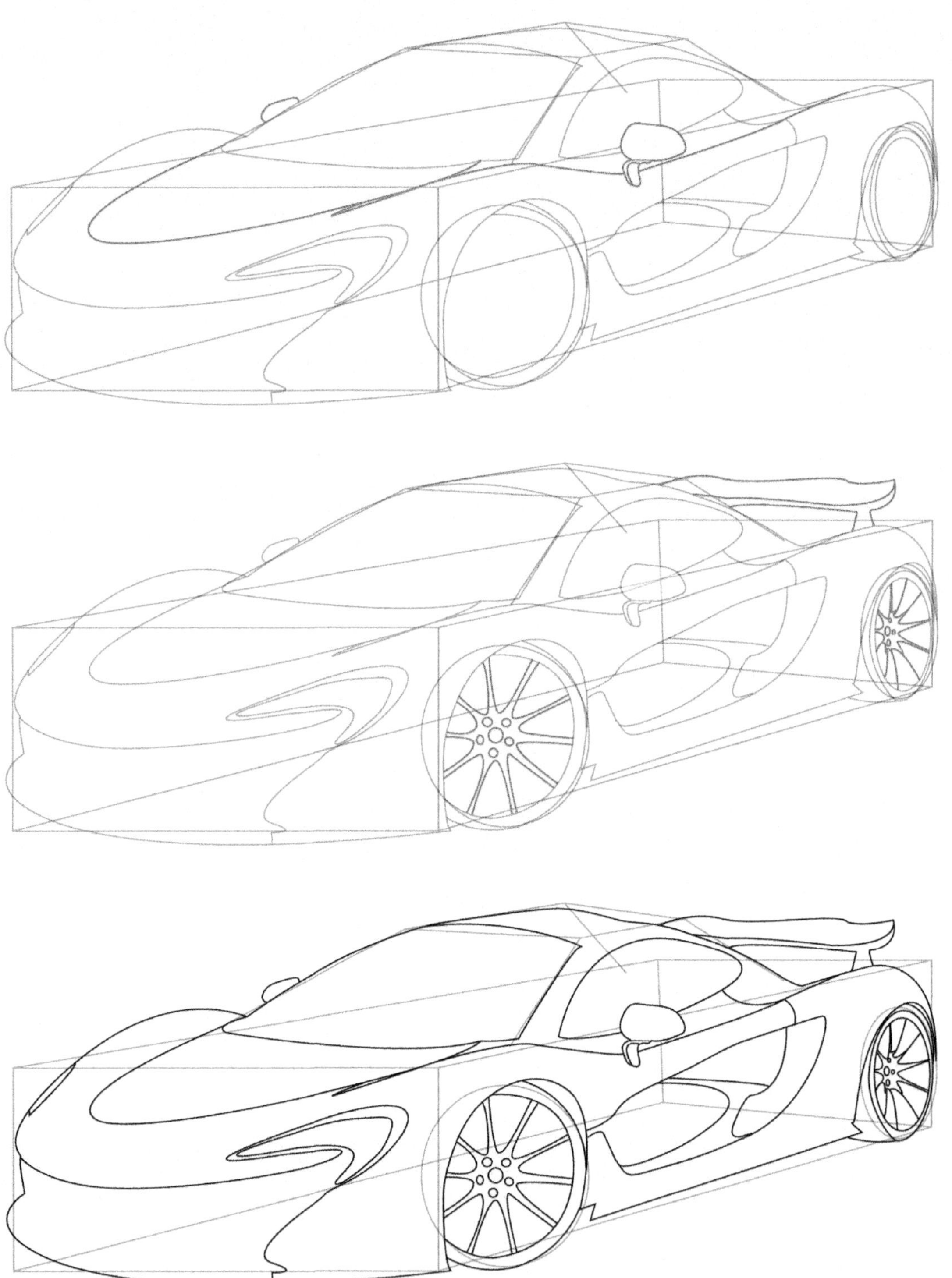

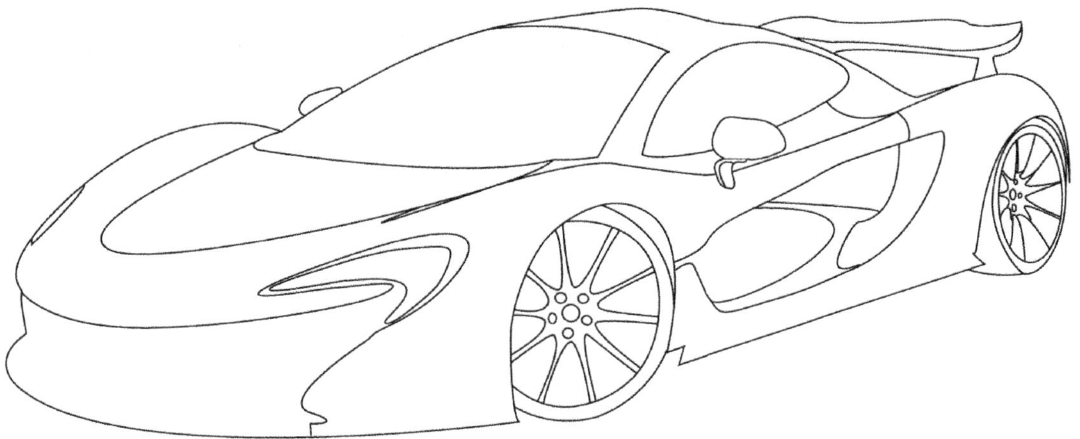

Dodge Challenger SRT

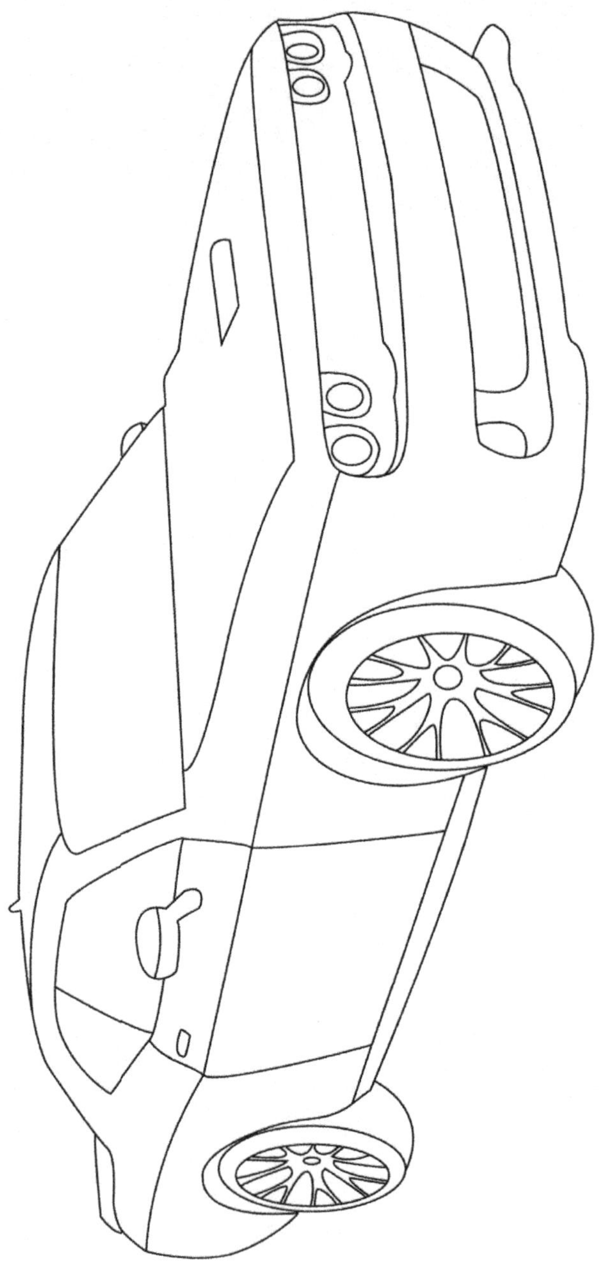

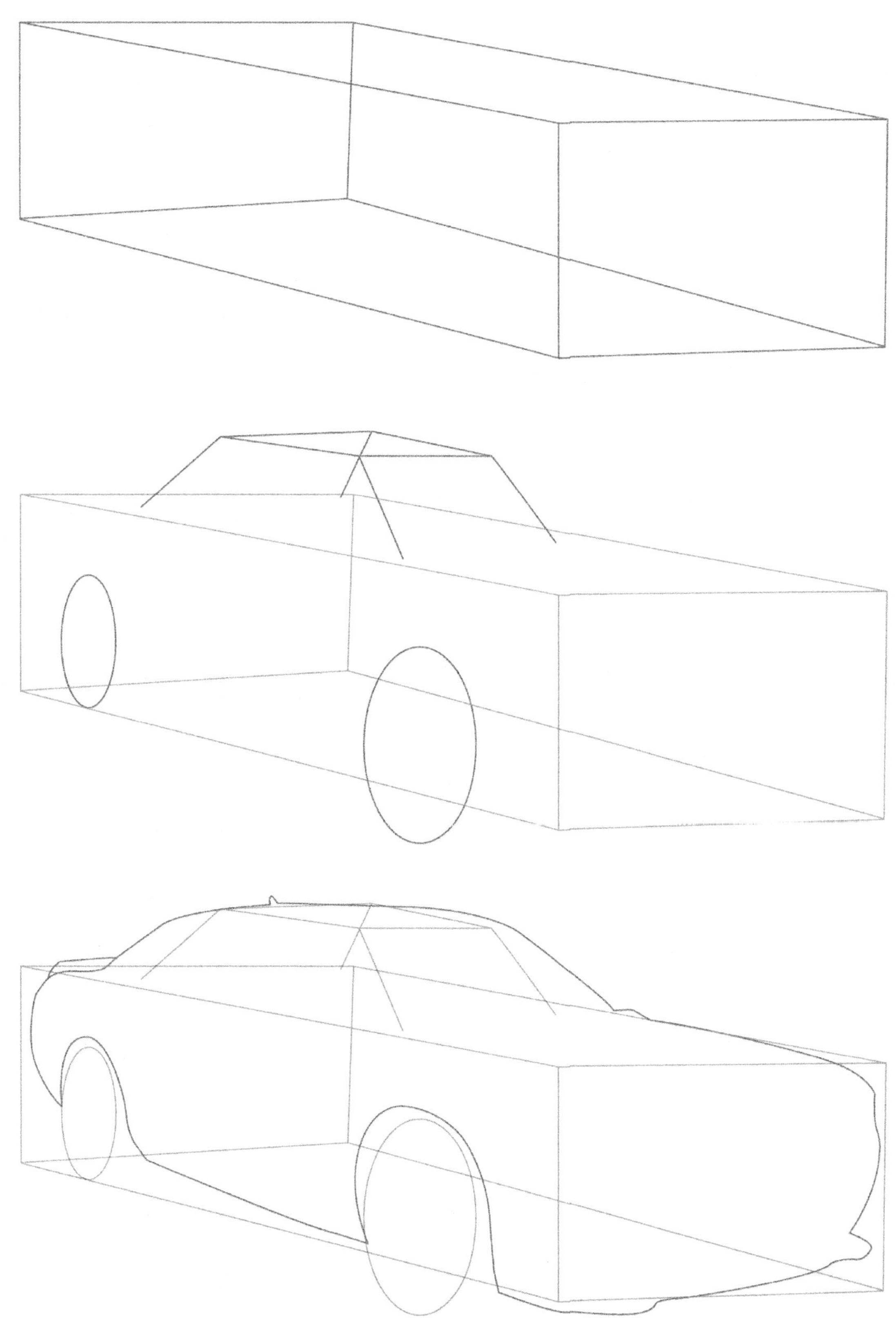

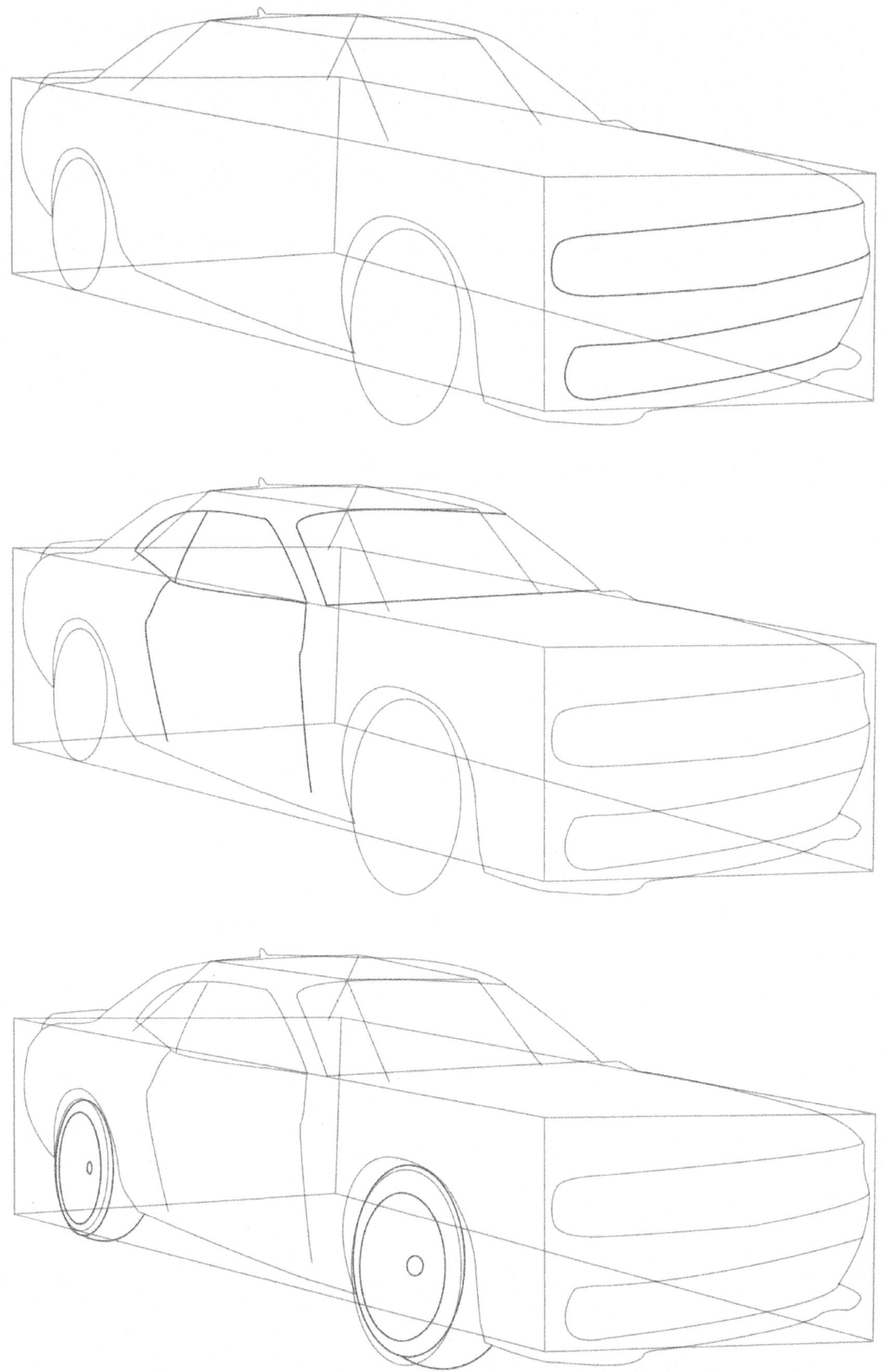

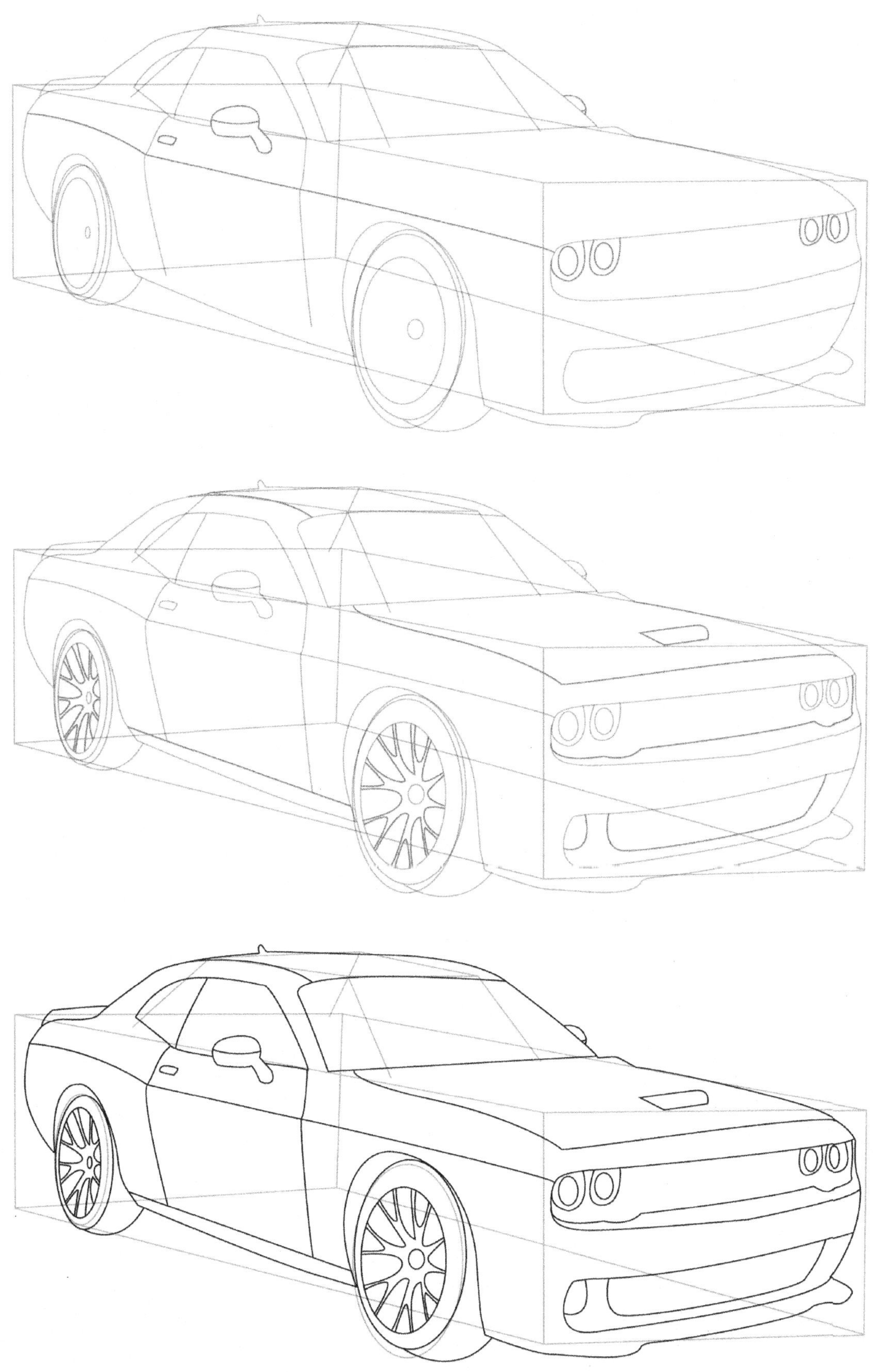

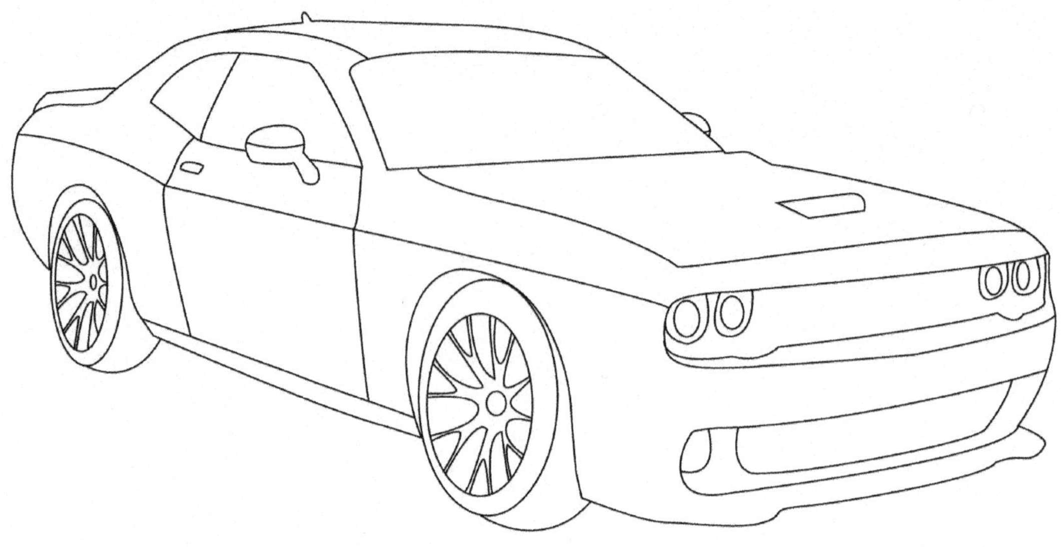

Bugatti Veyron 16.4 Grand Sport

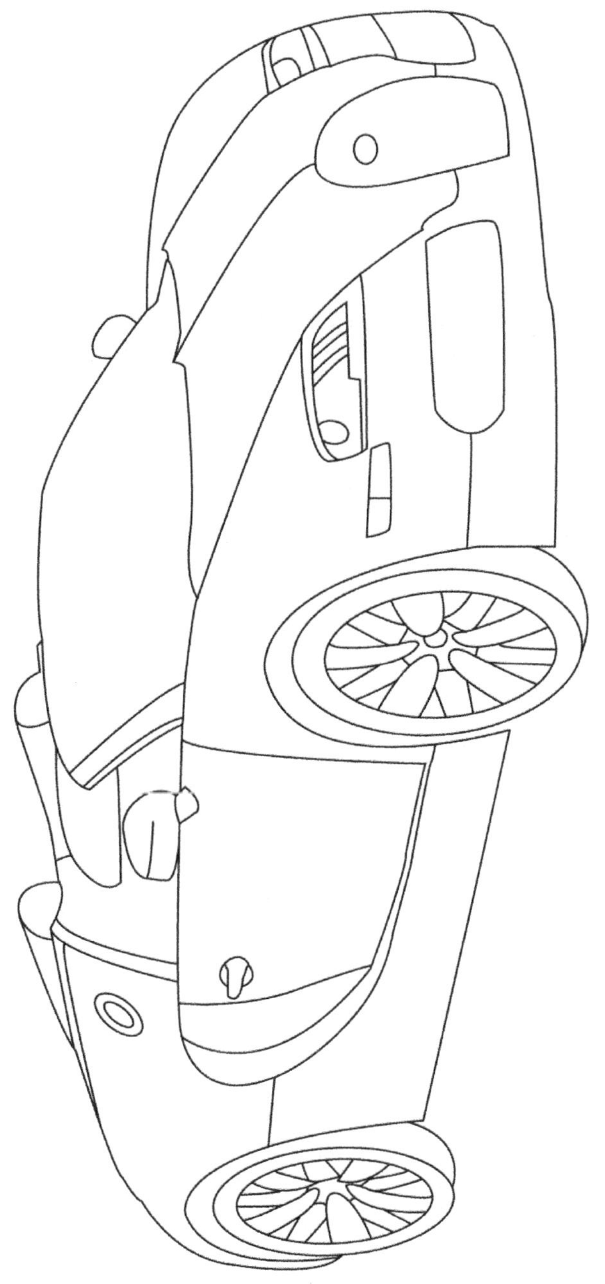

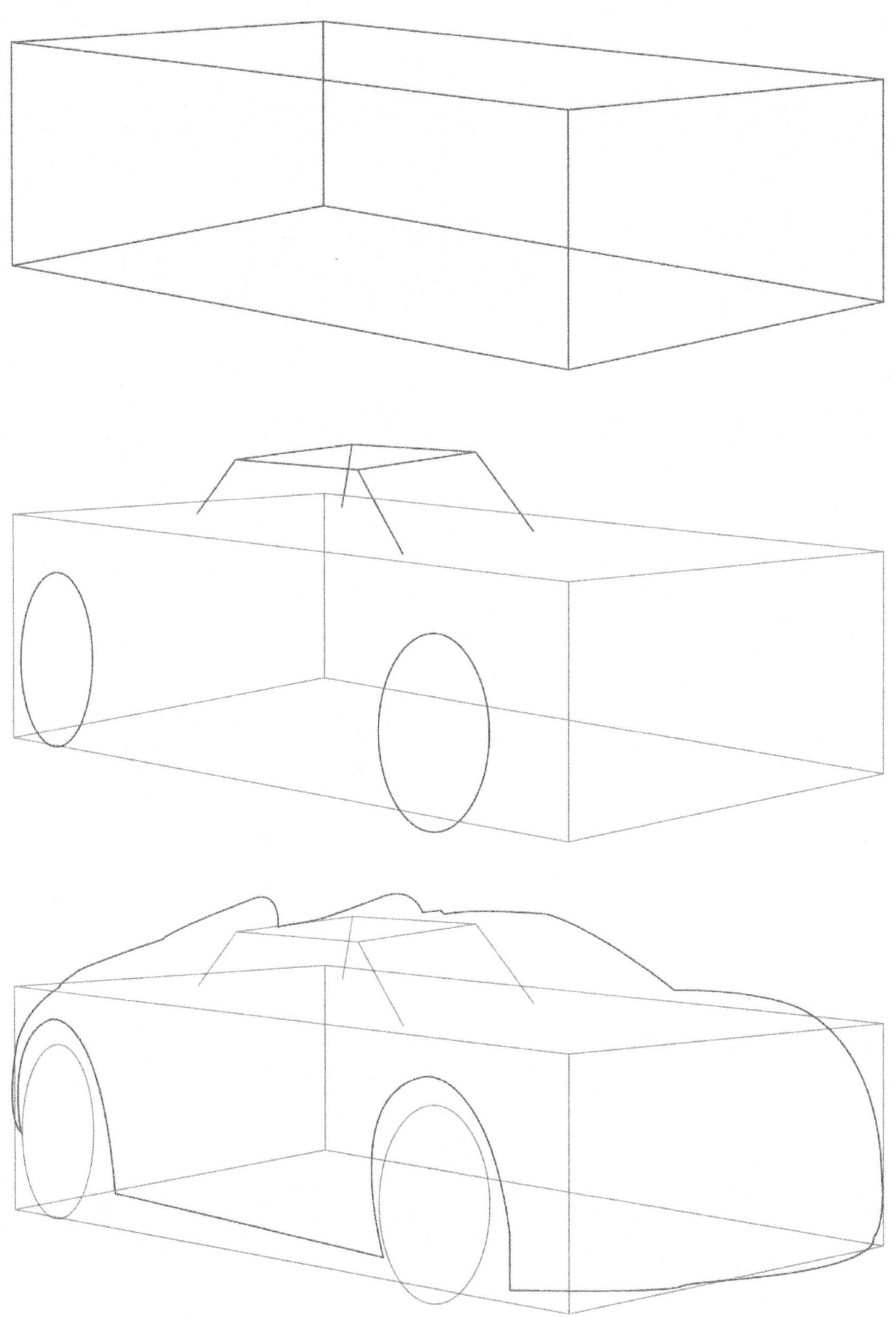

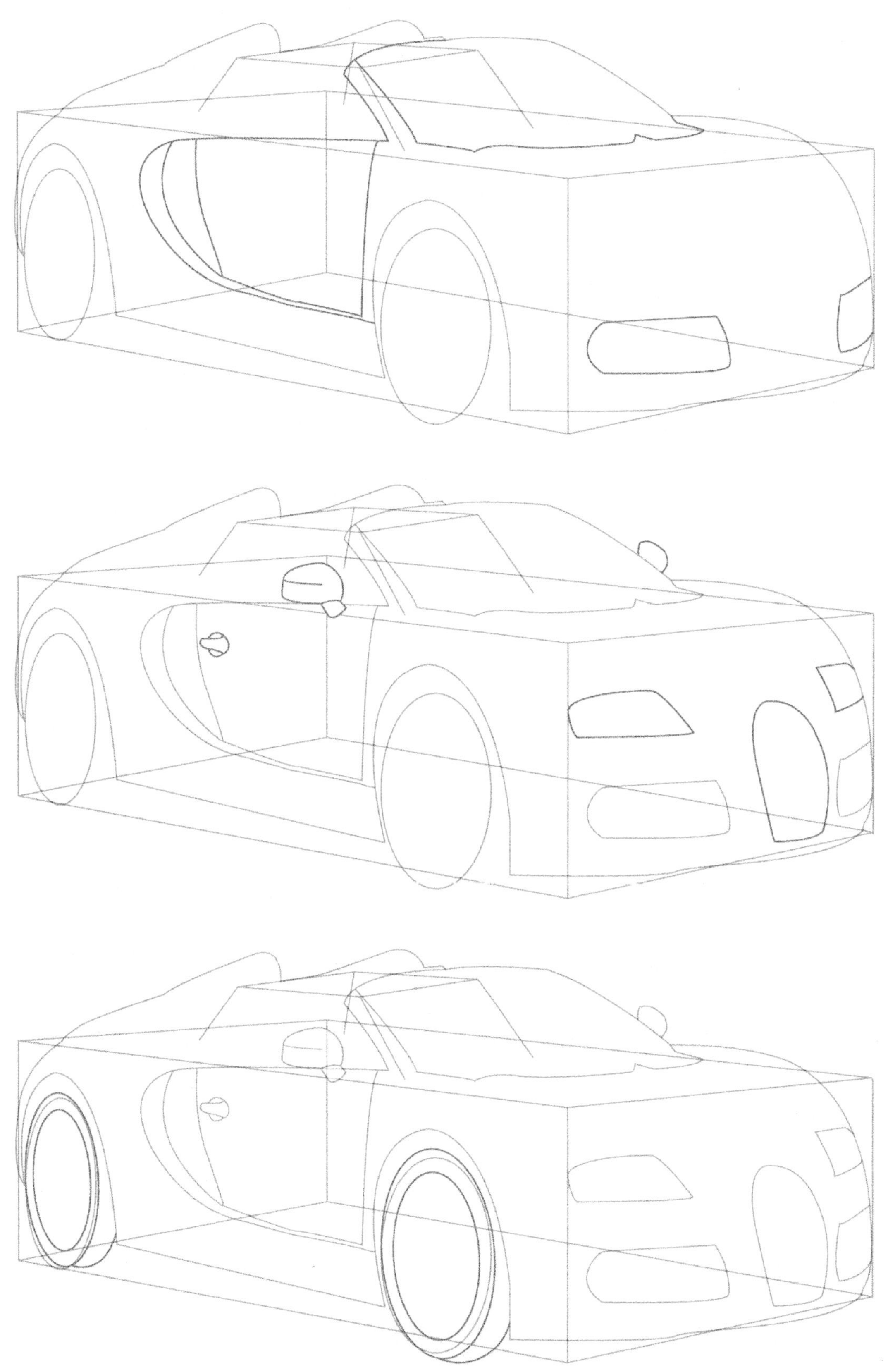

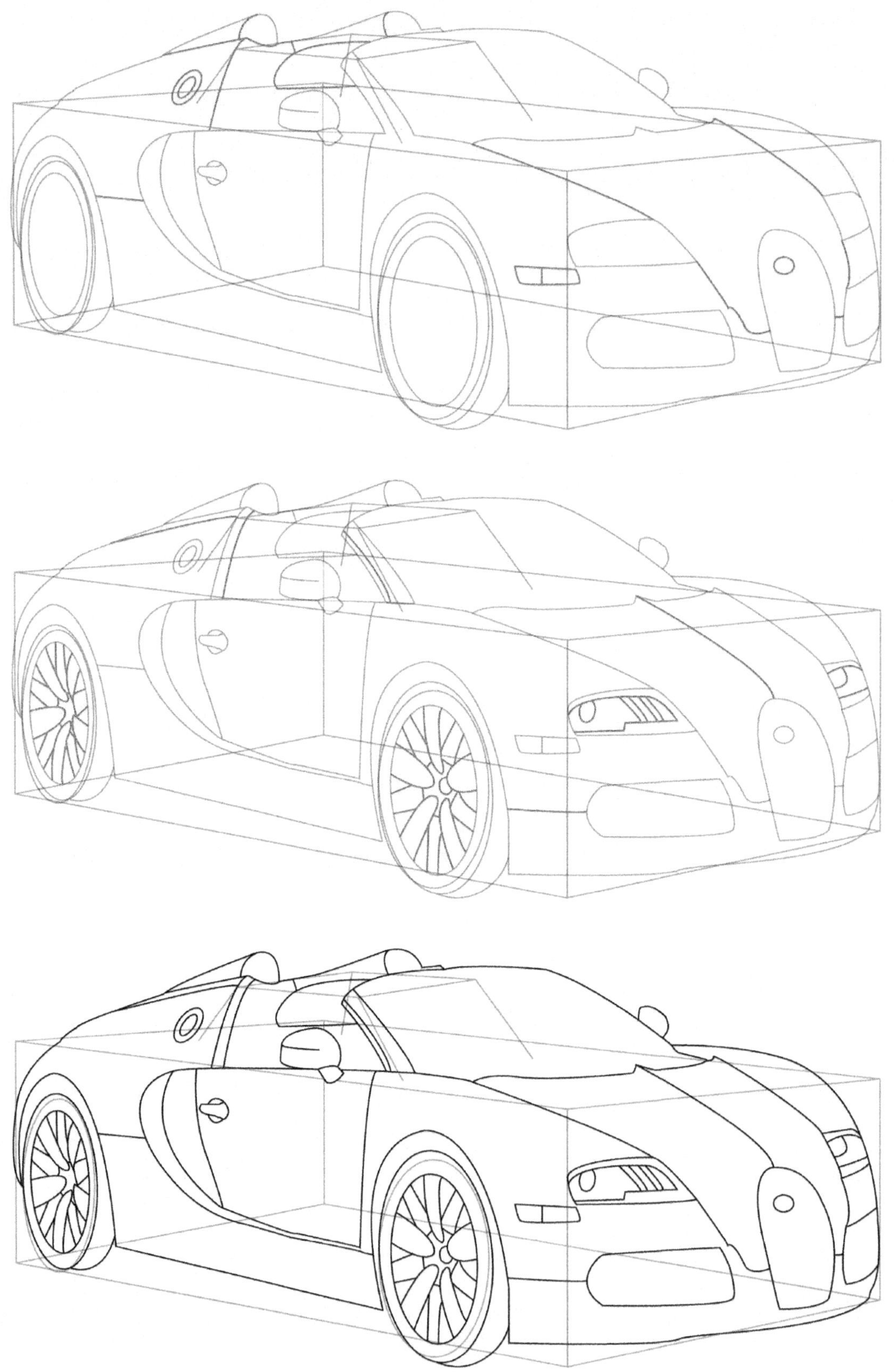

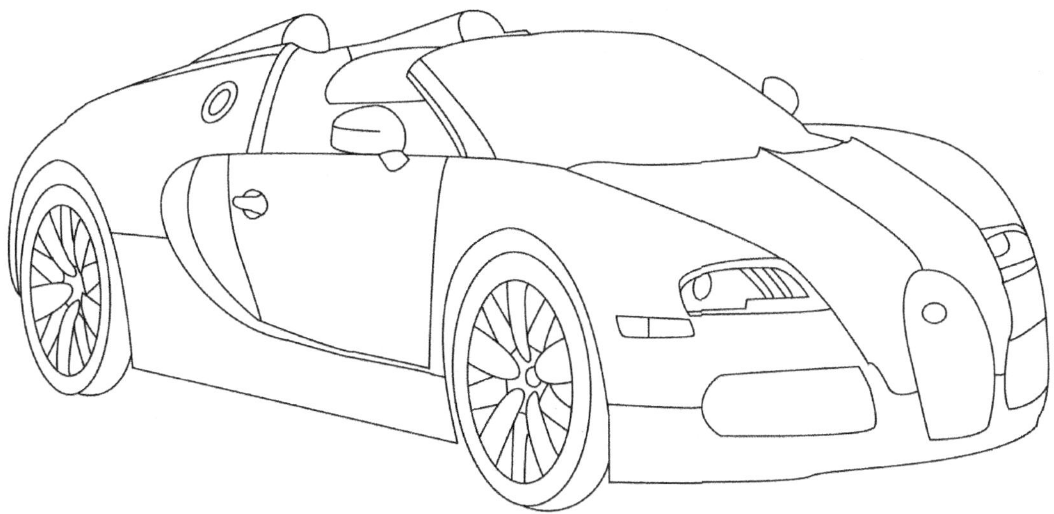

Chevrolet Corvette Stingray 2020

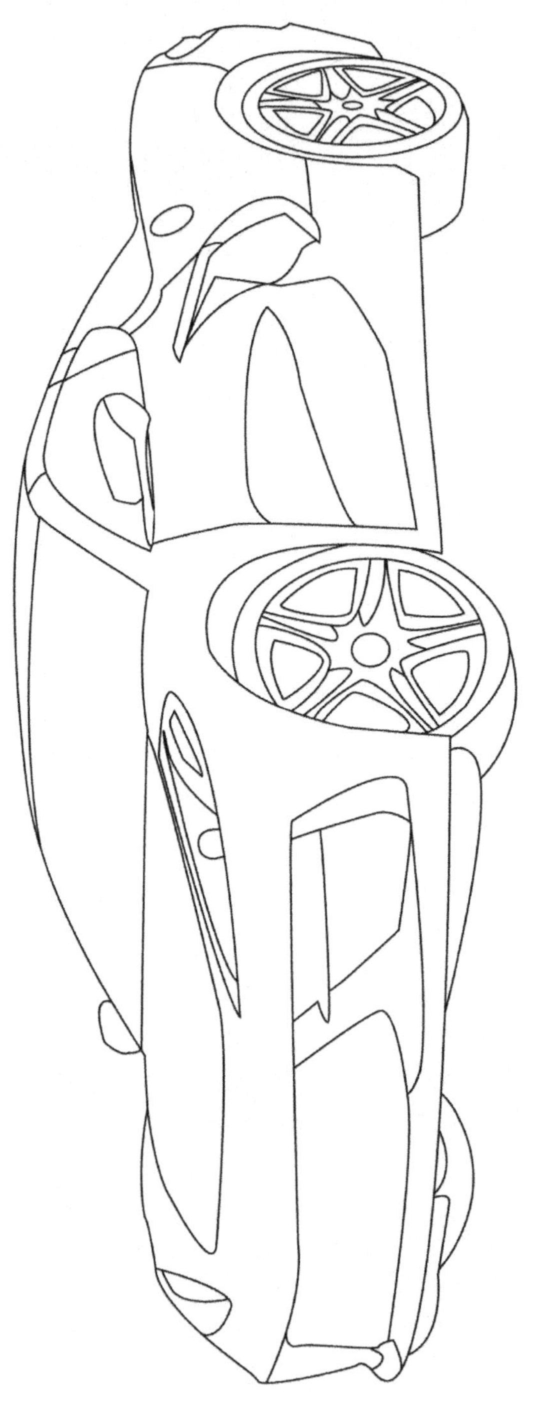

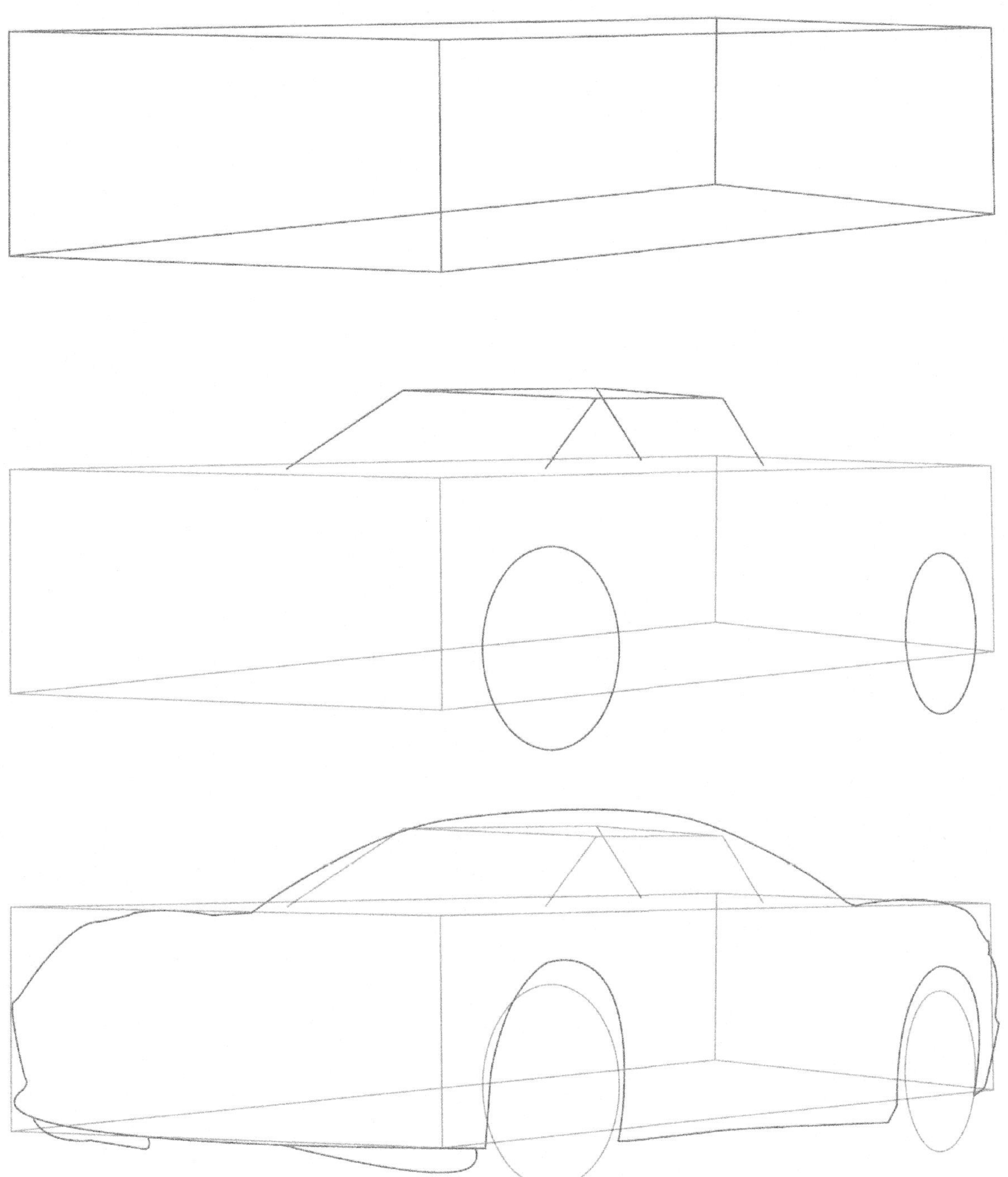

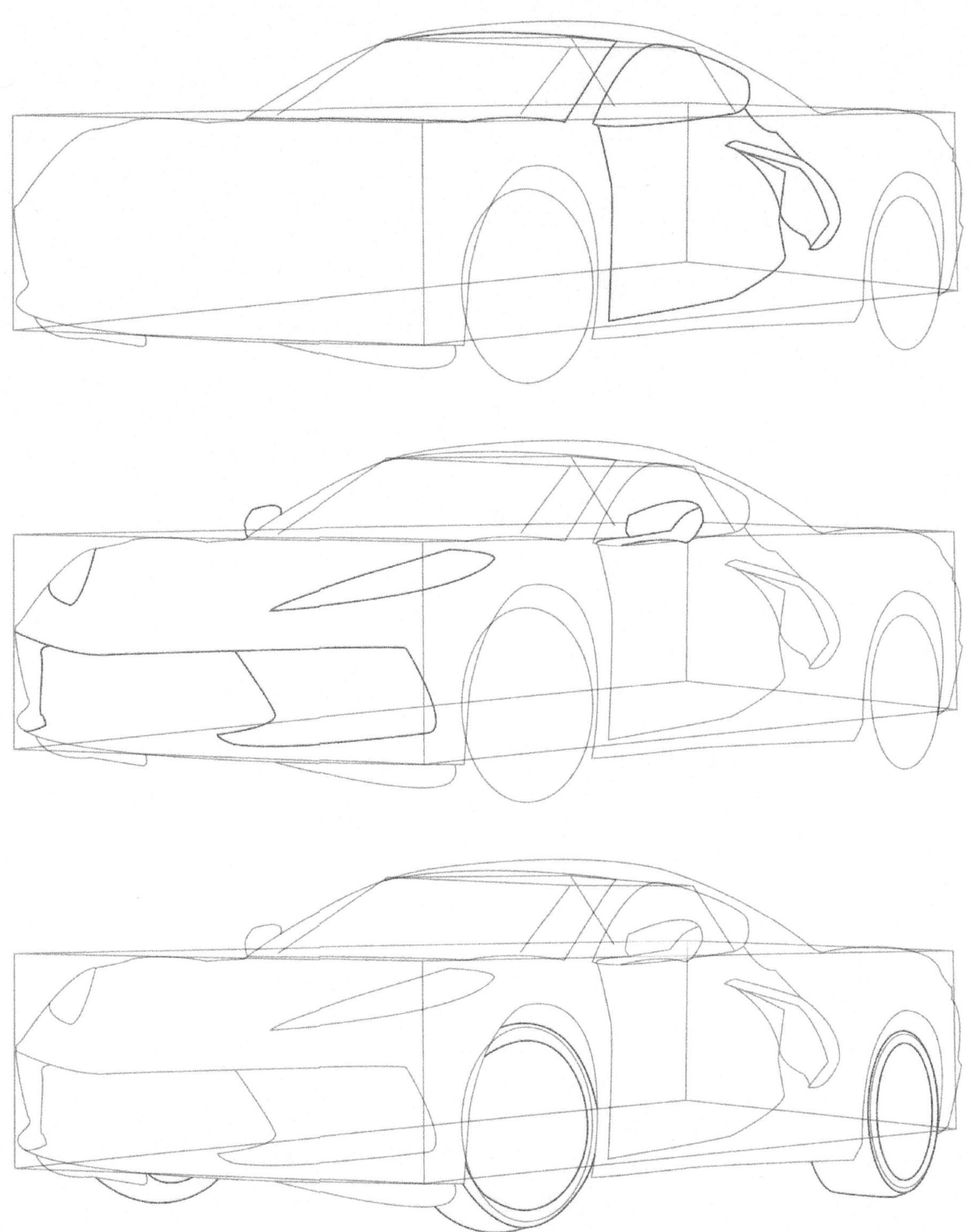

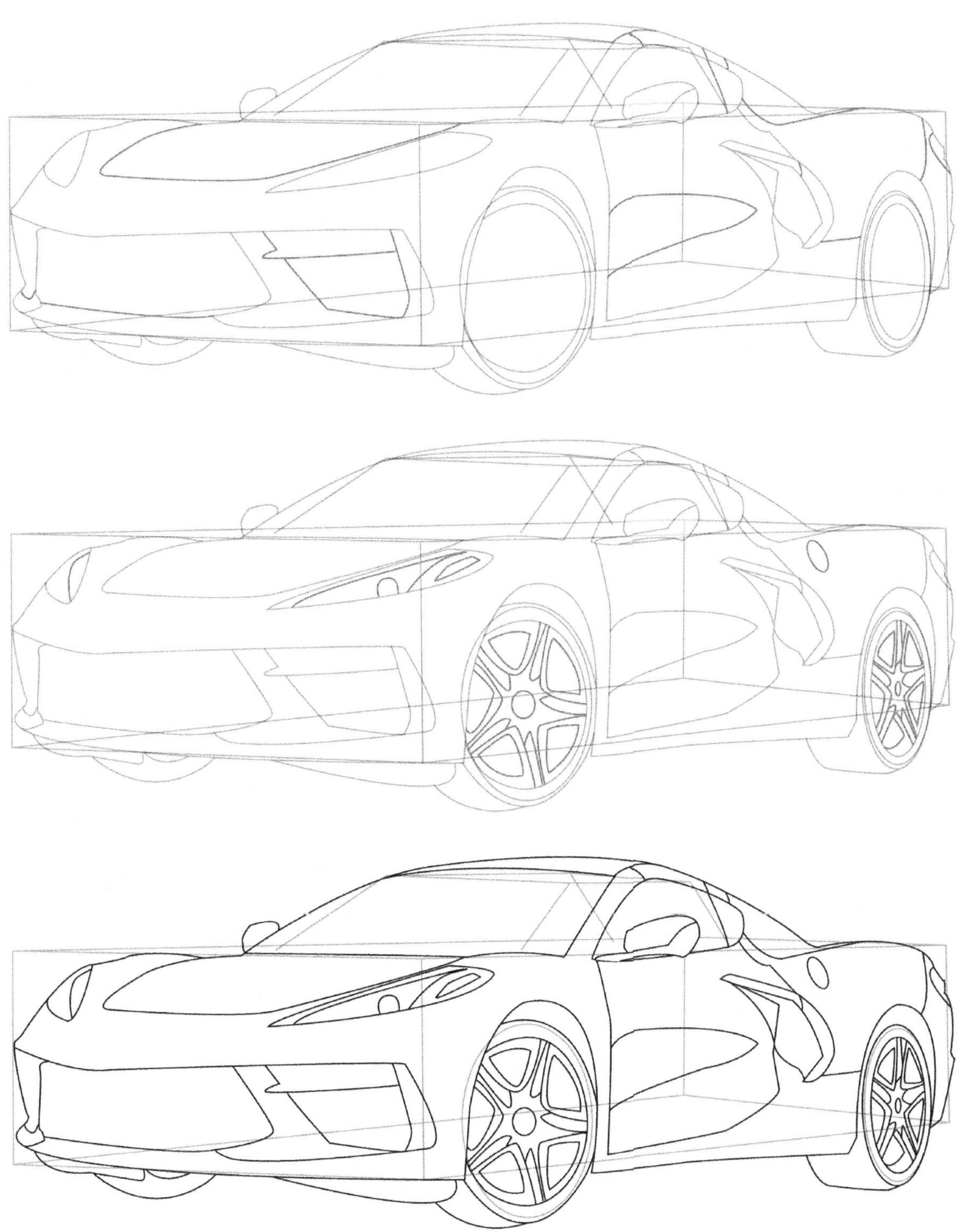

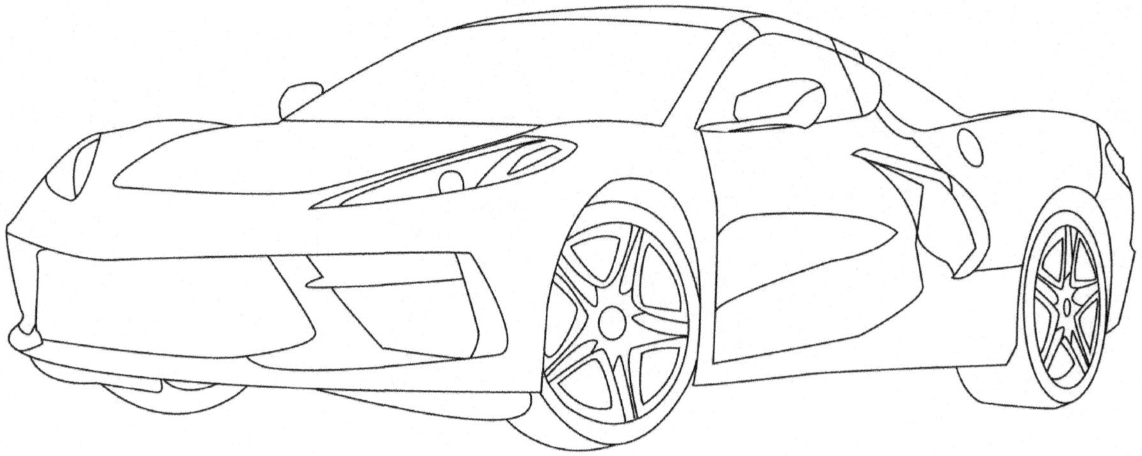

Chevrolet Corvette Stingray 1967

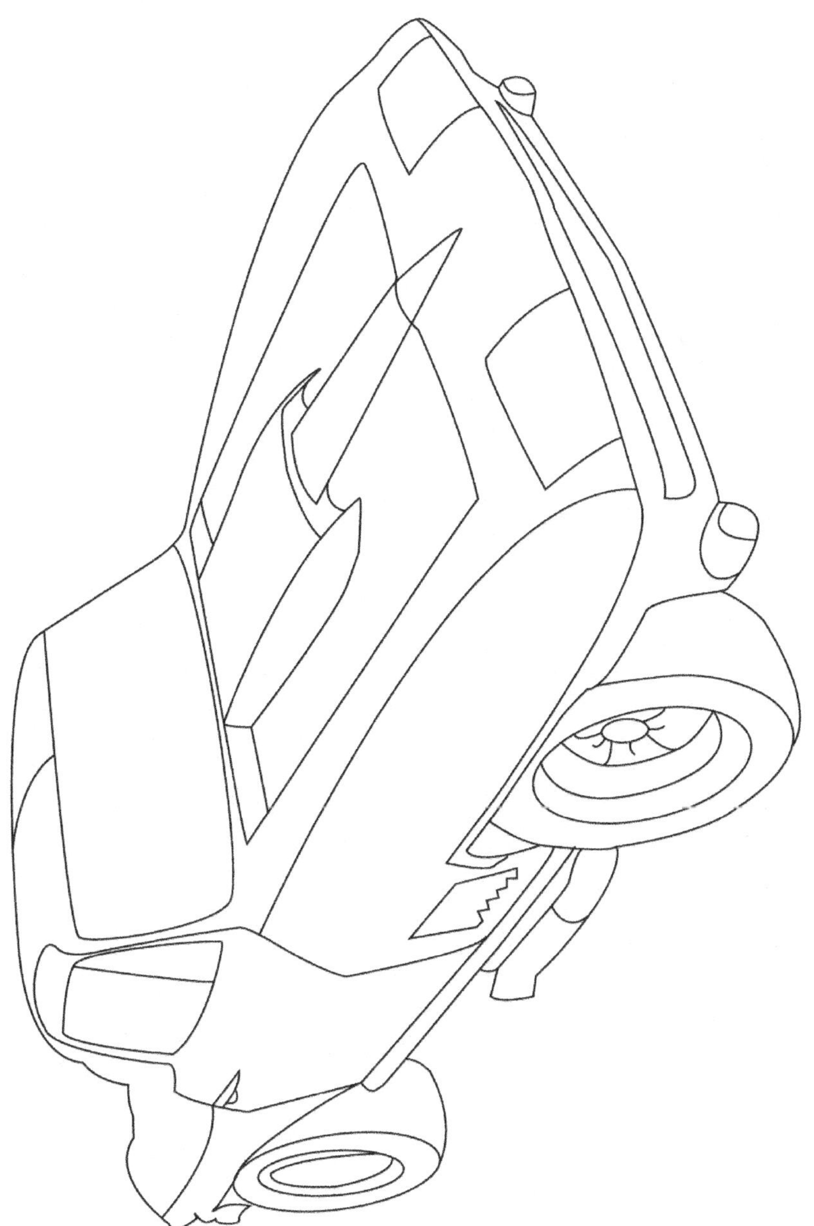

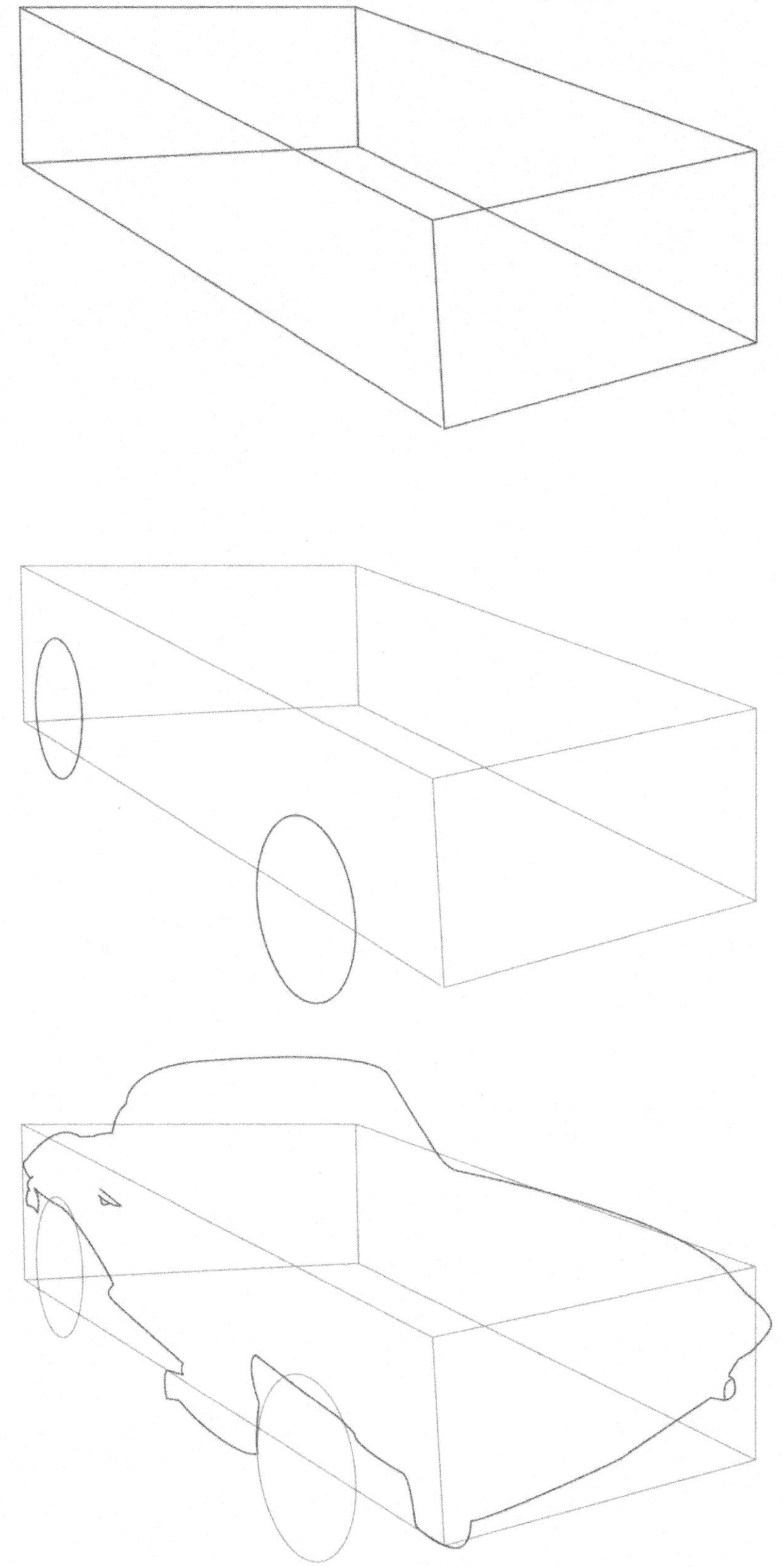

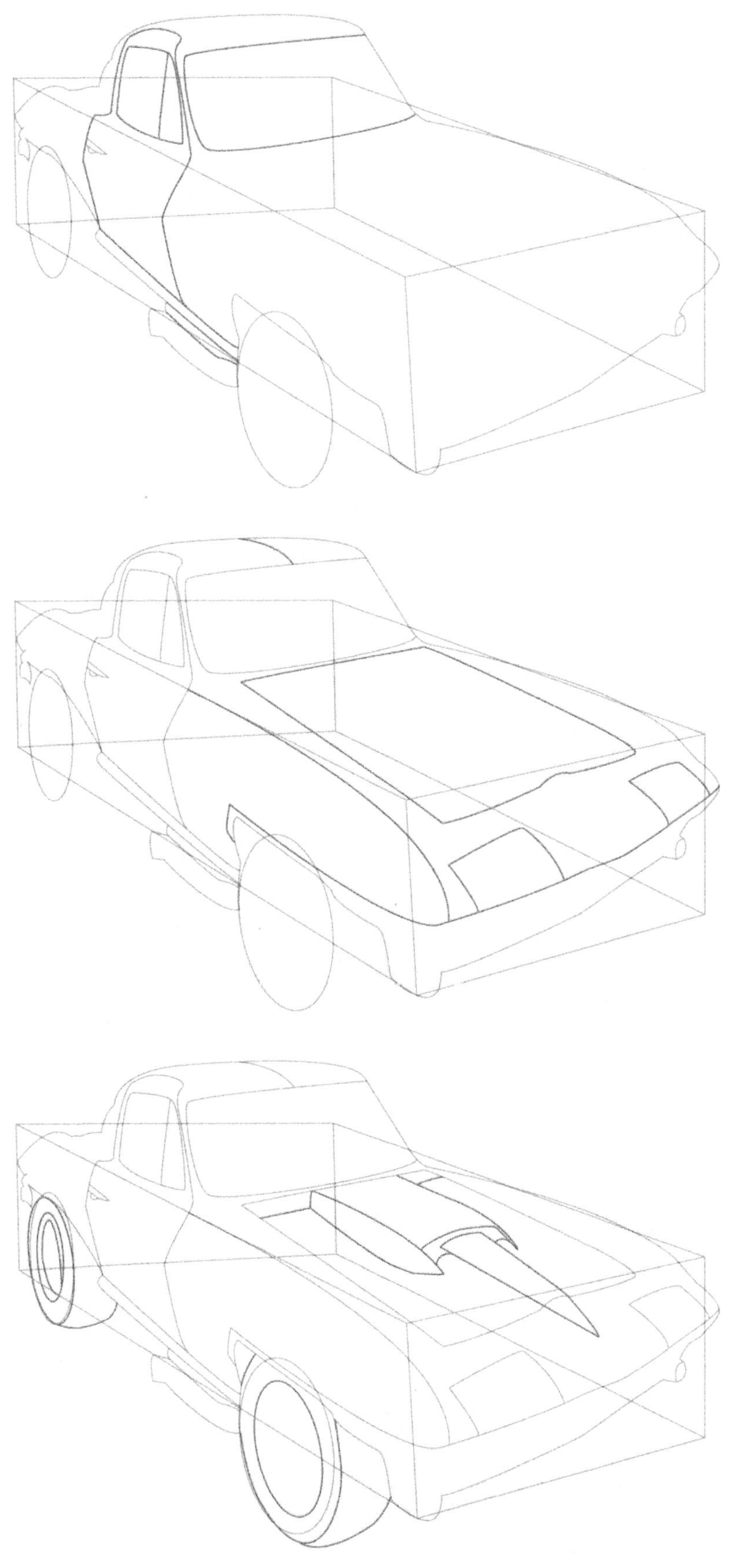

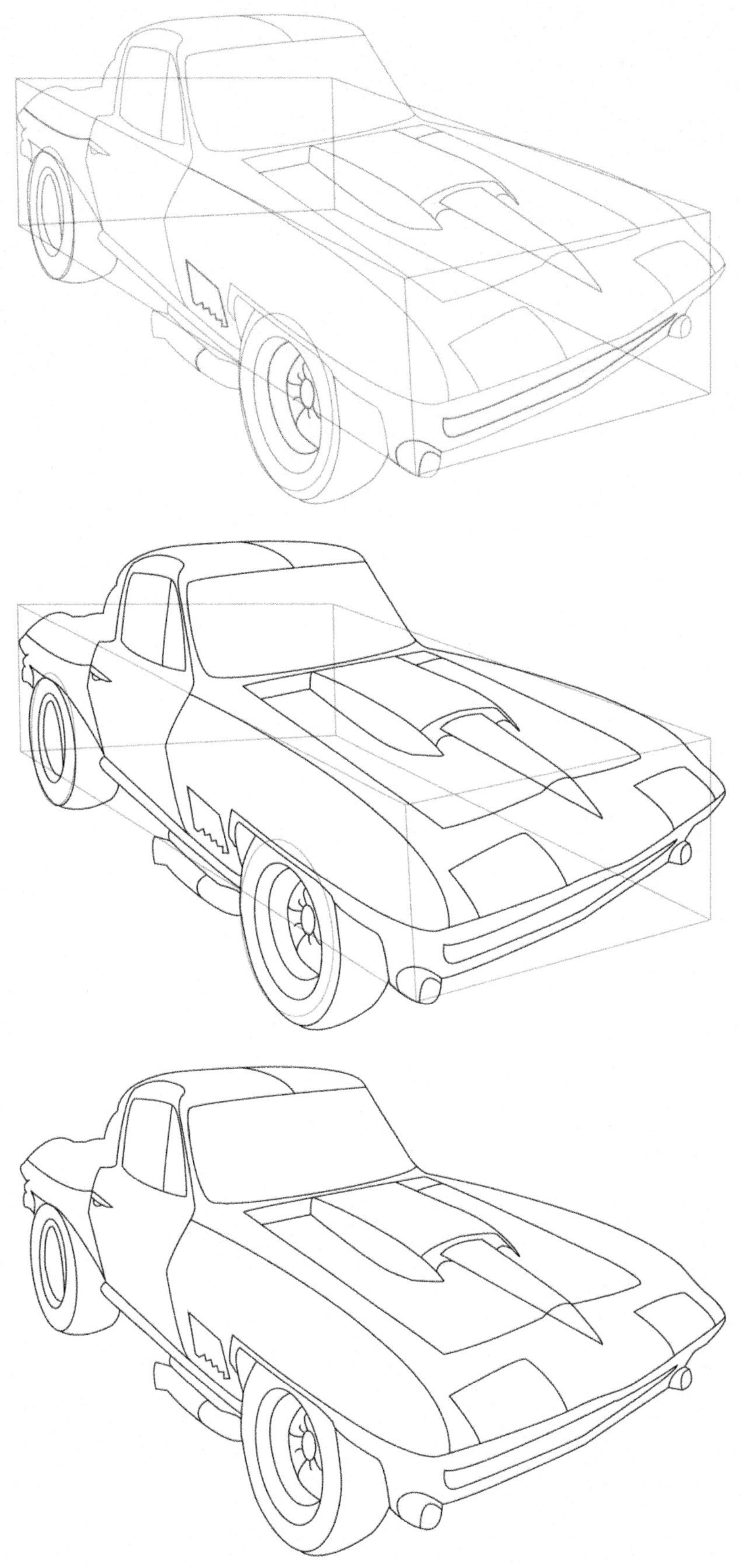

Dodge Ram 2500

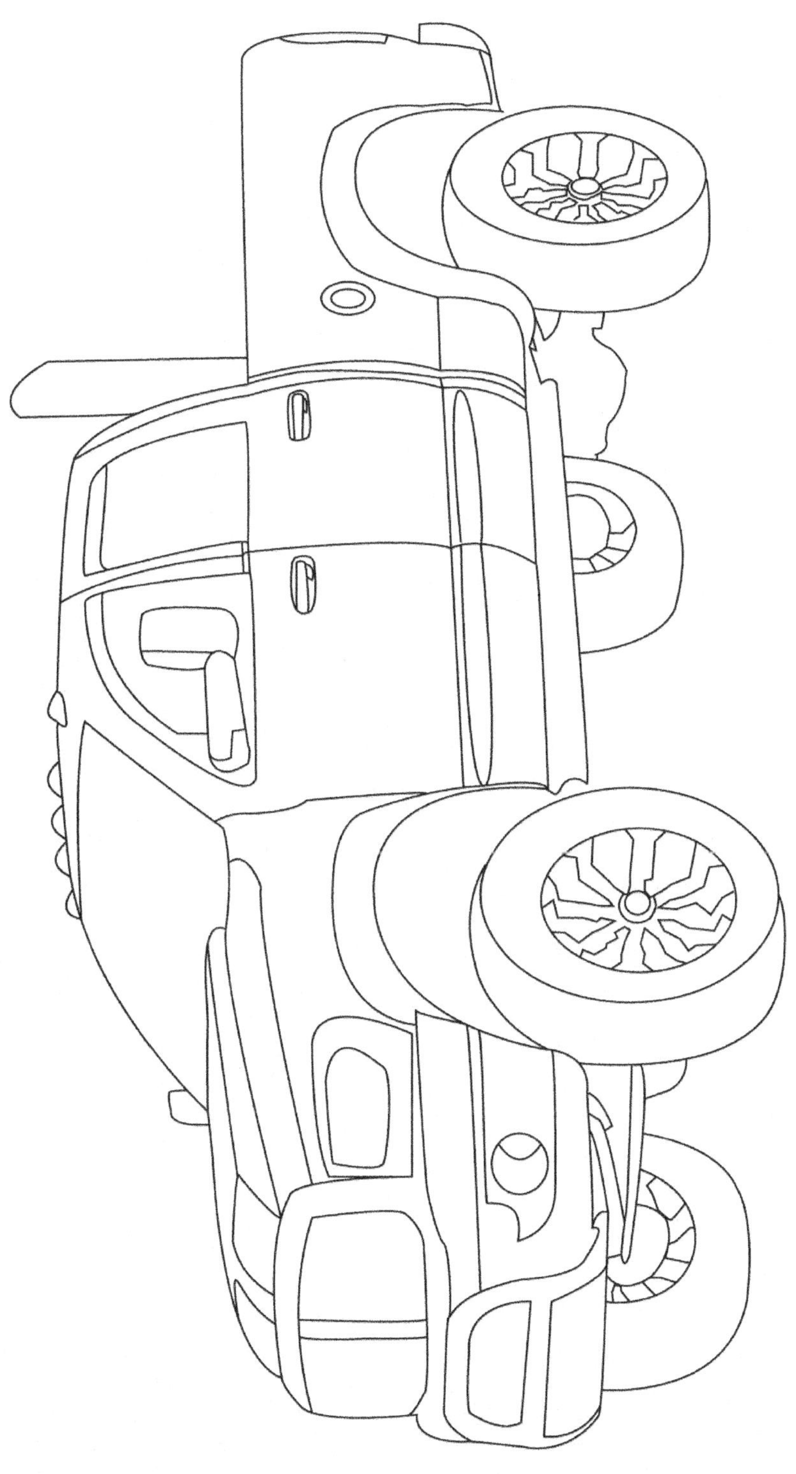

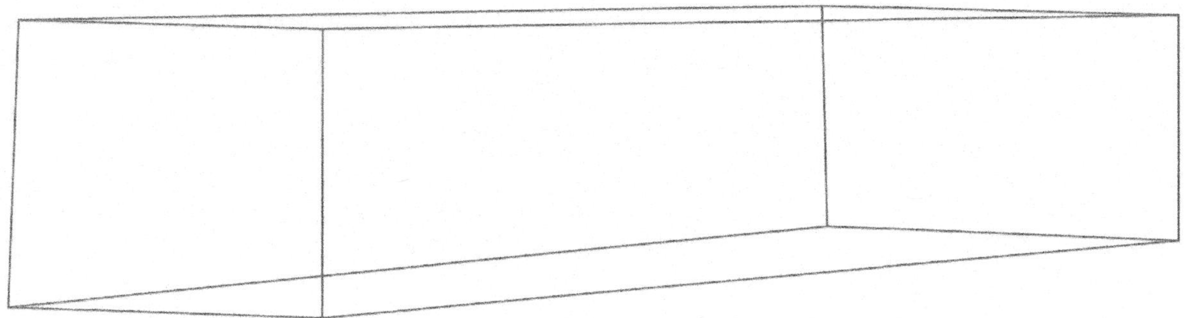

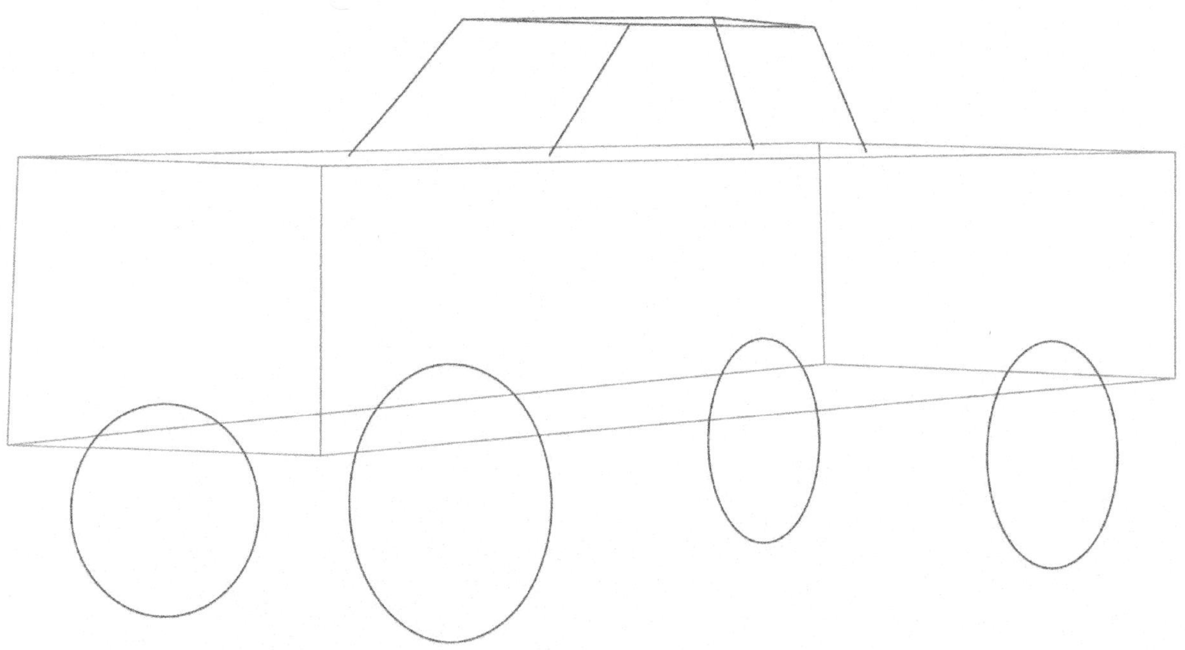

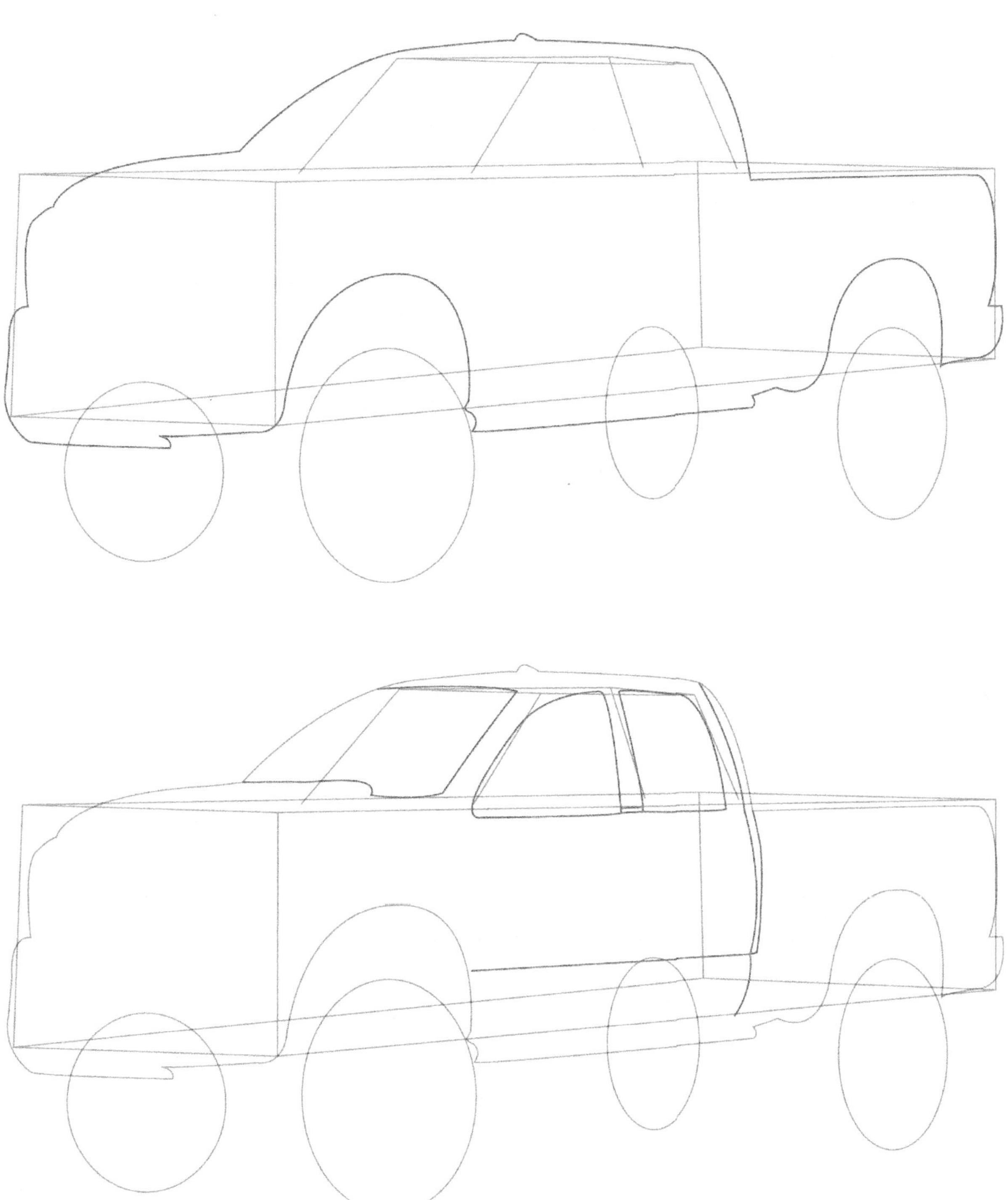

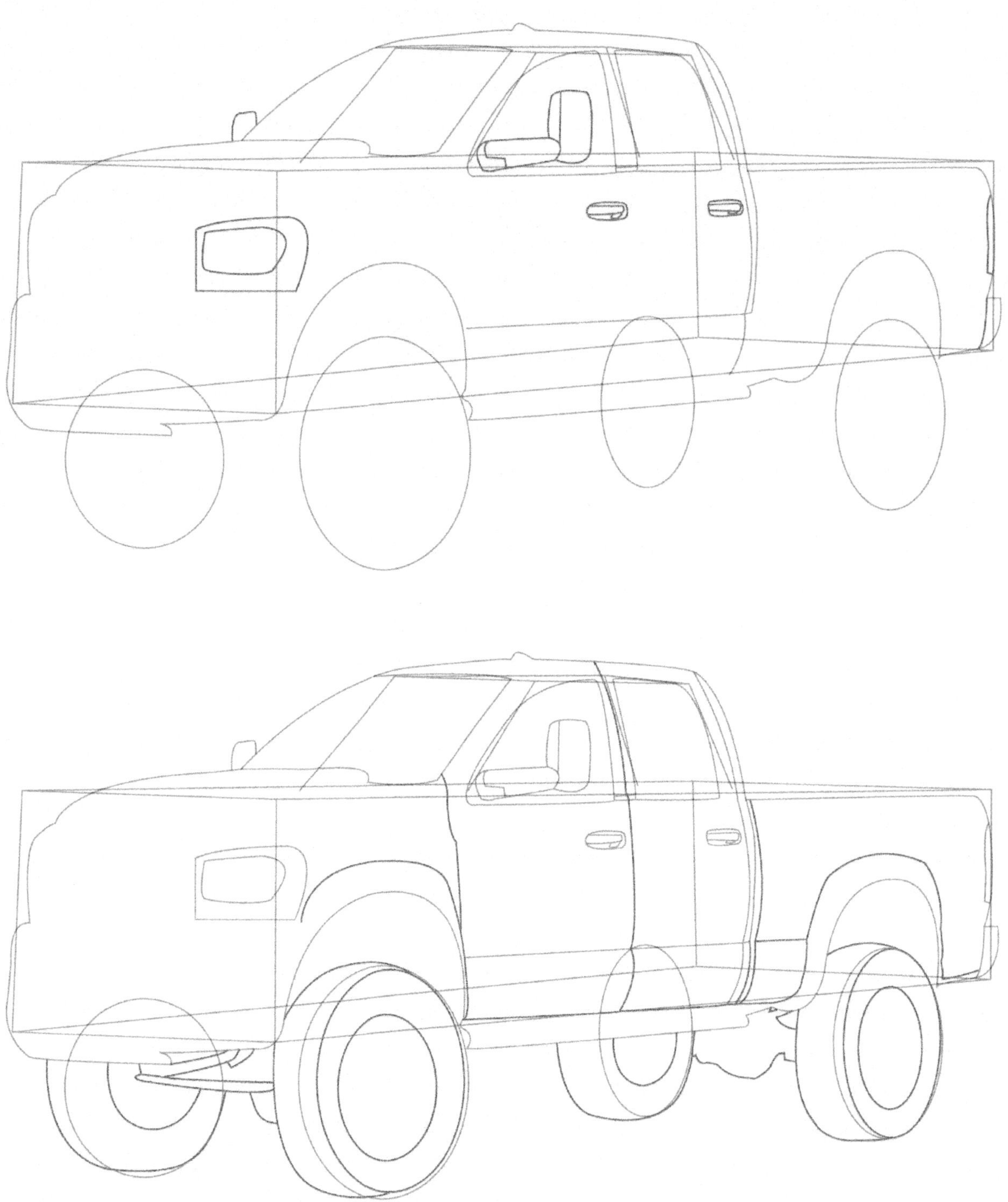

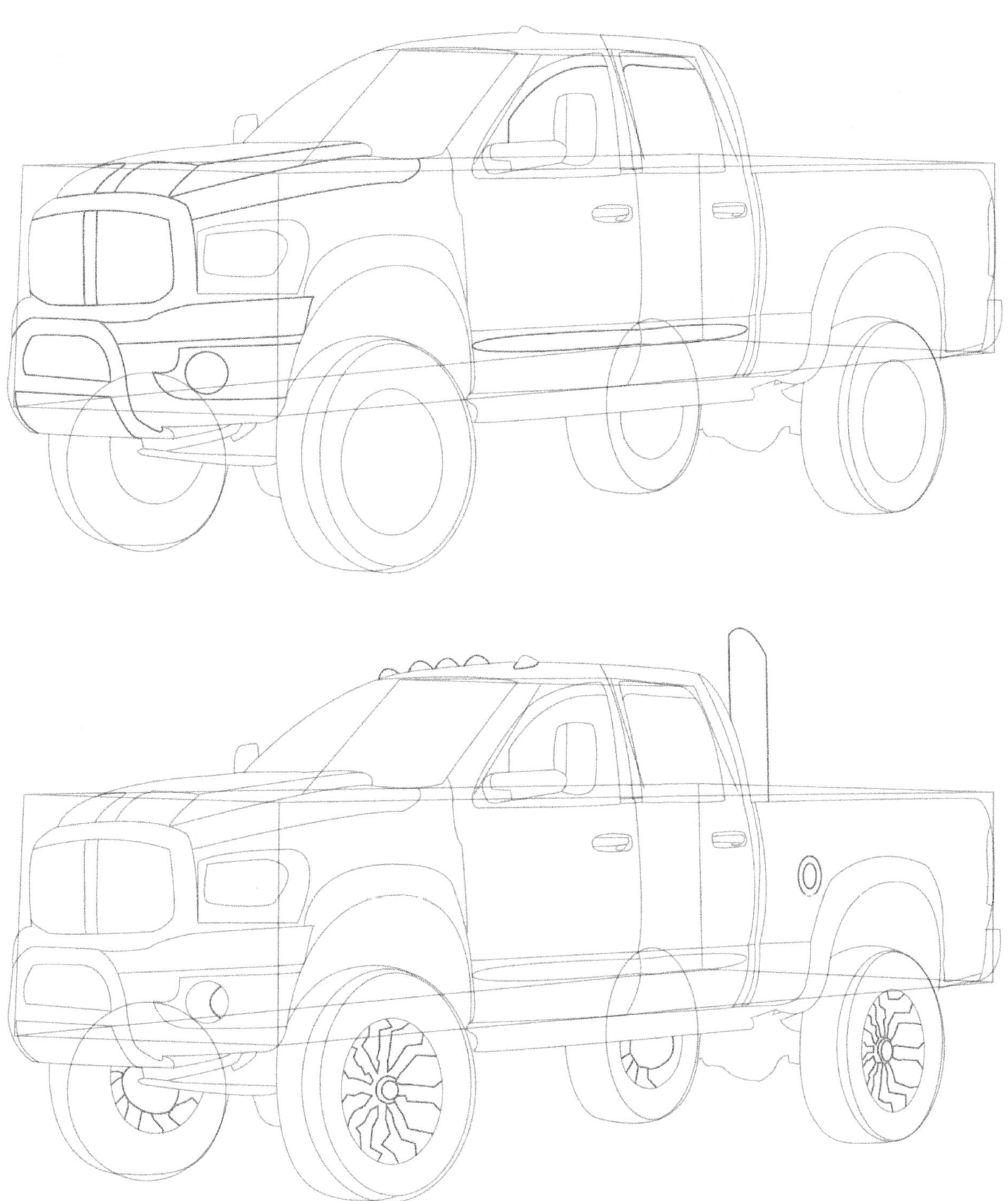

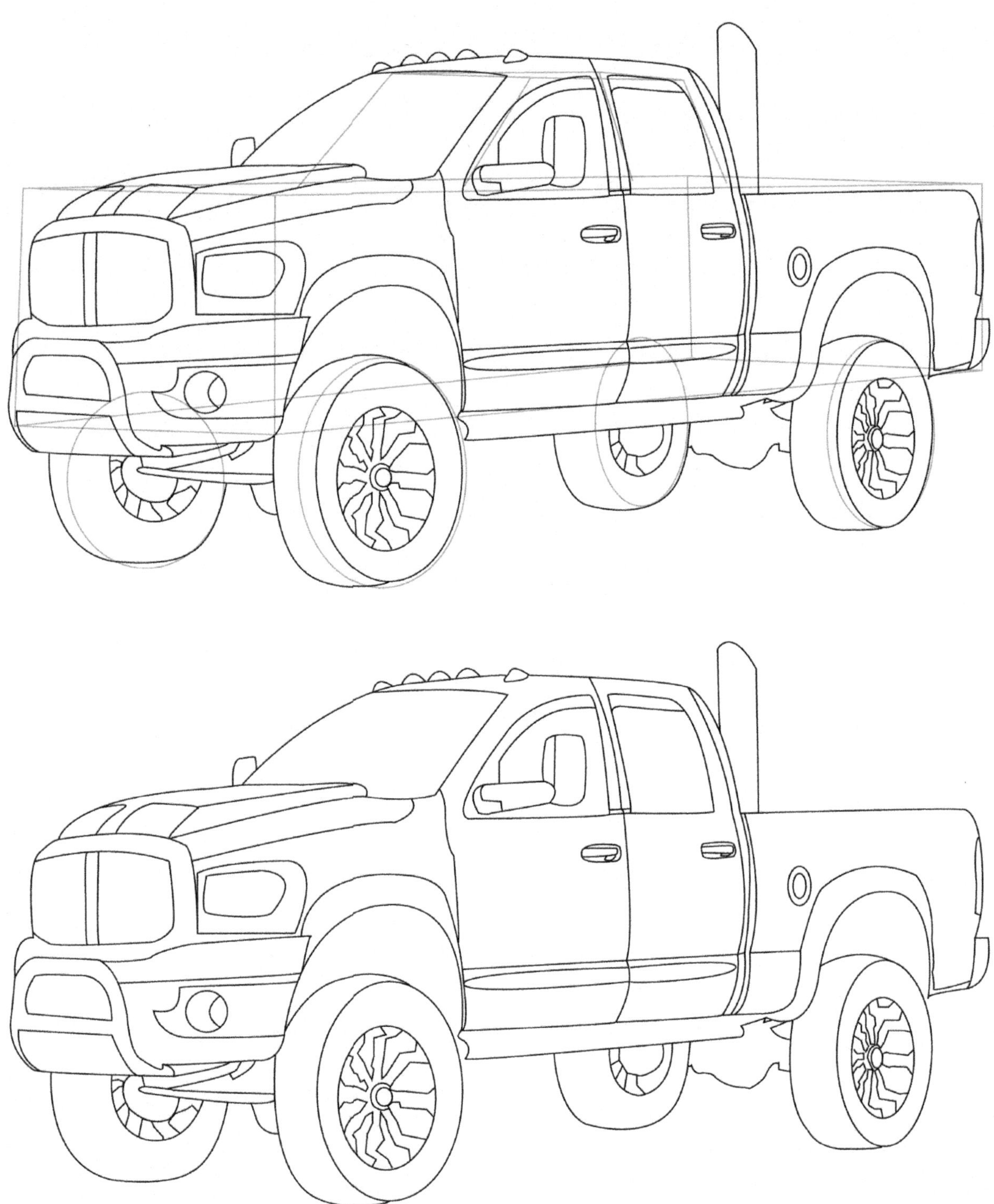

Ford Mustang Mach 1

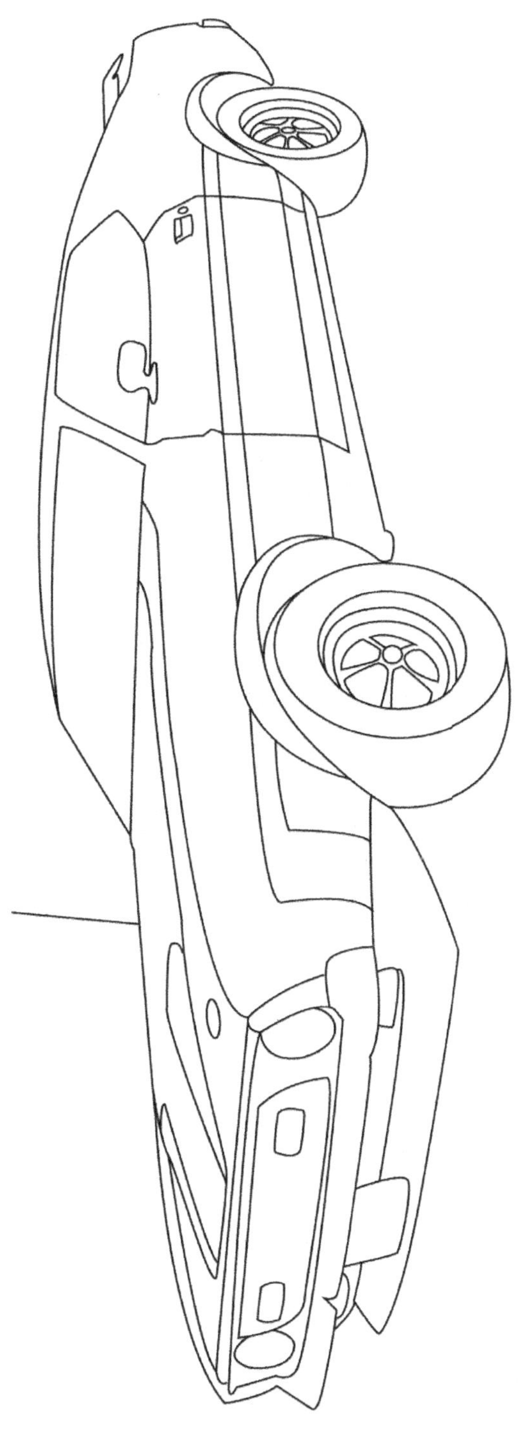

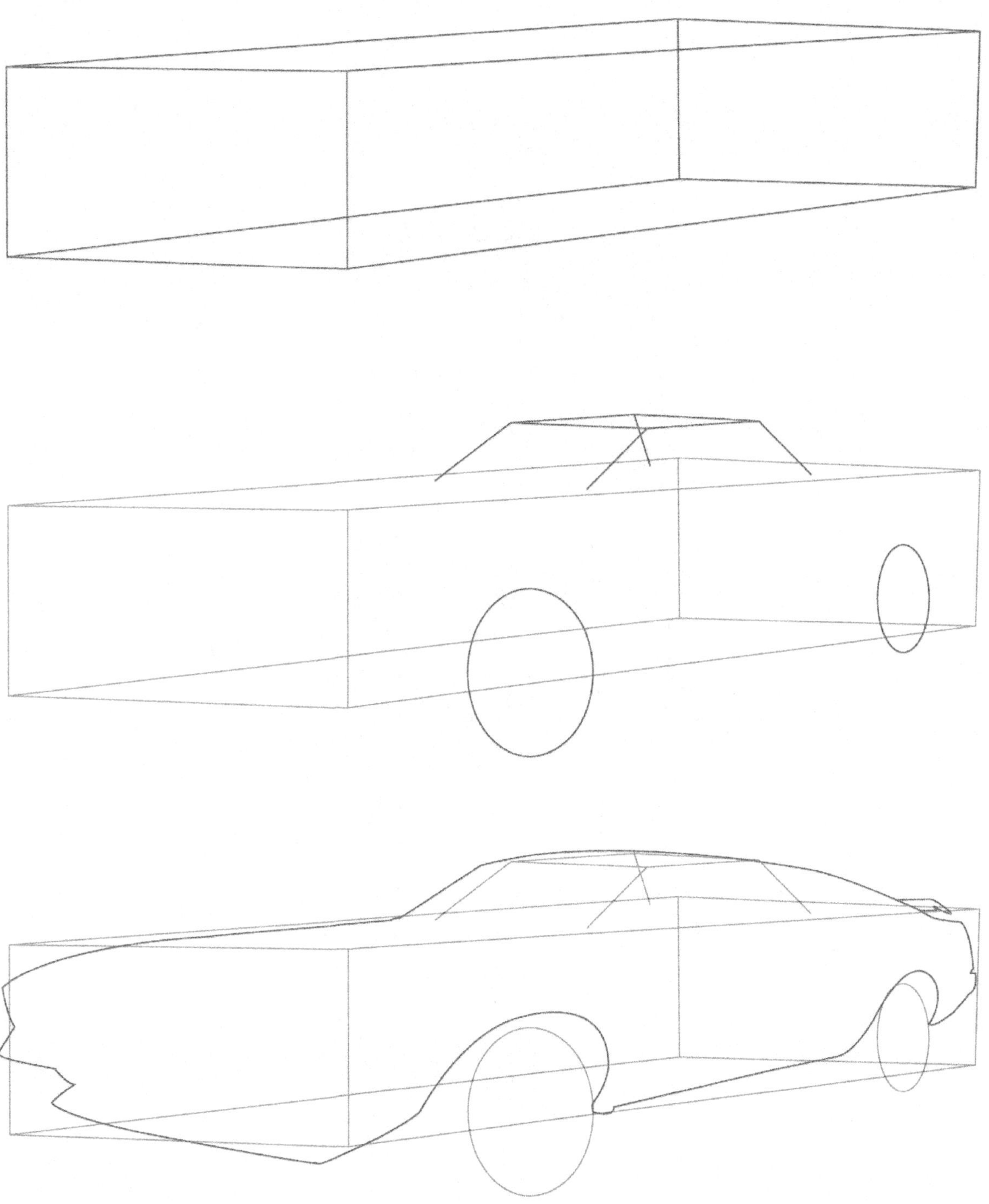

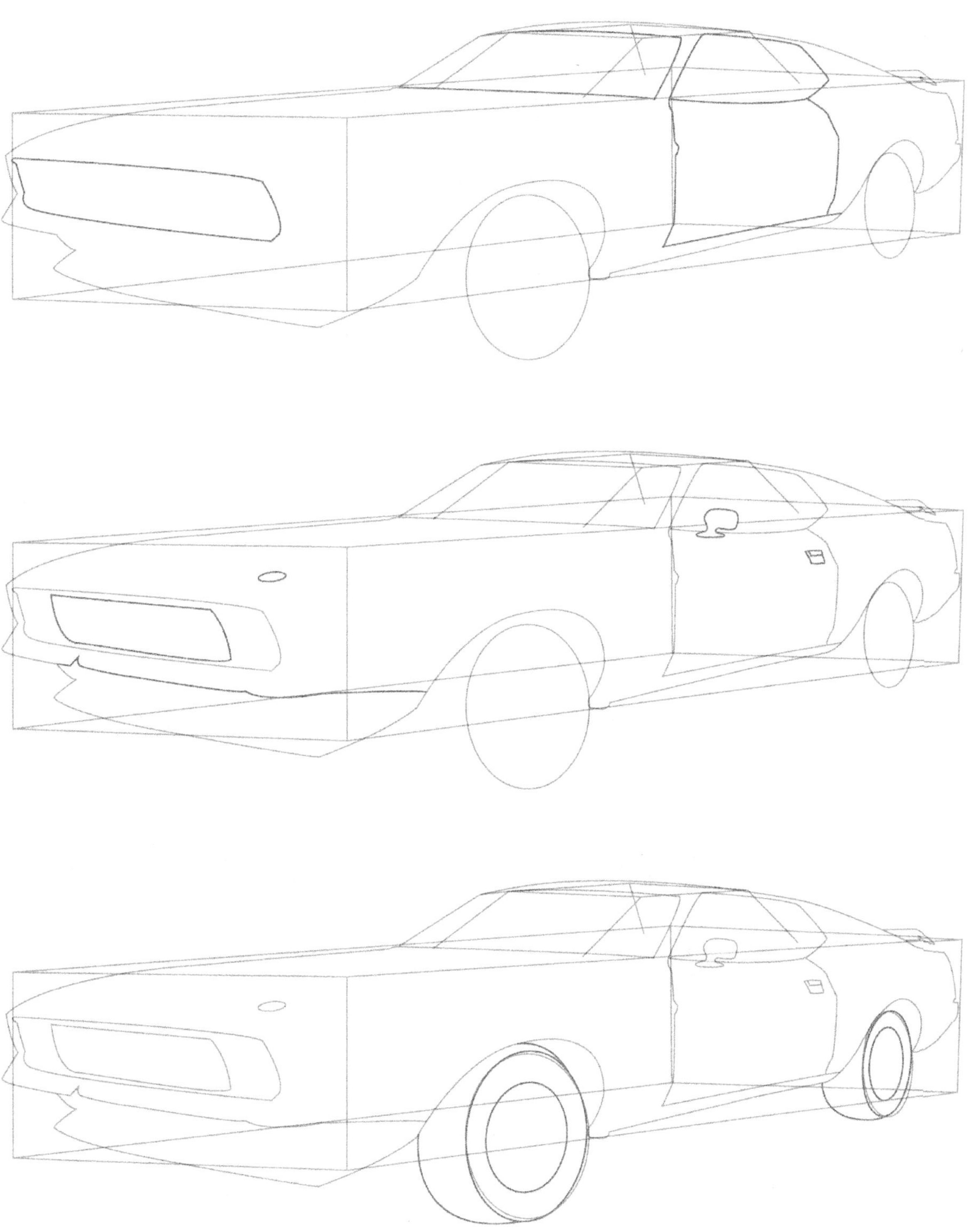

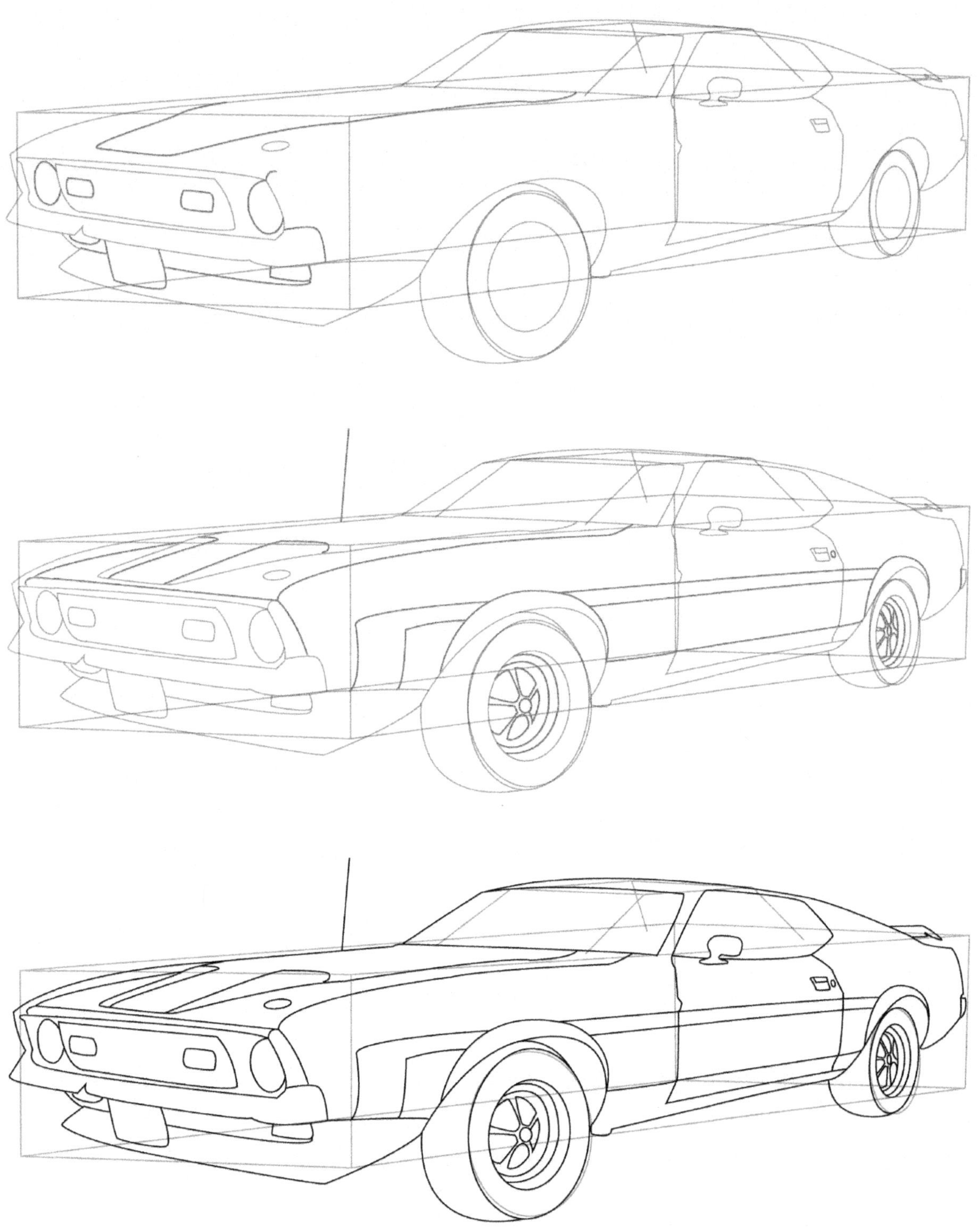

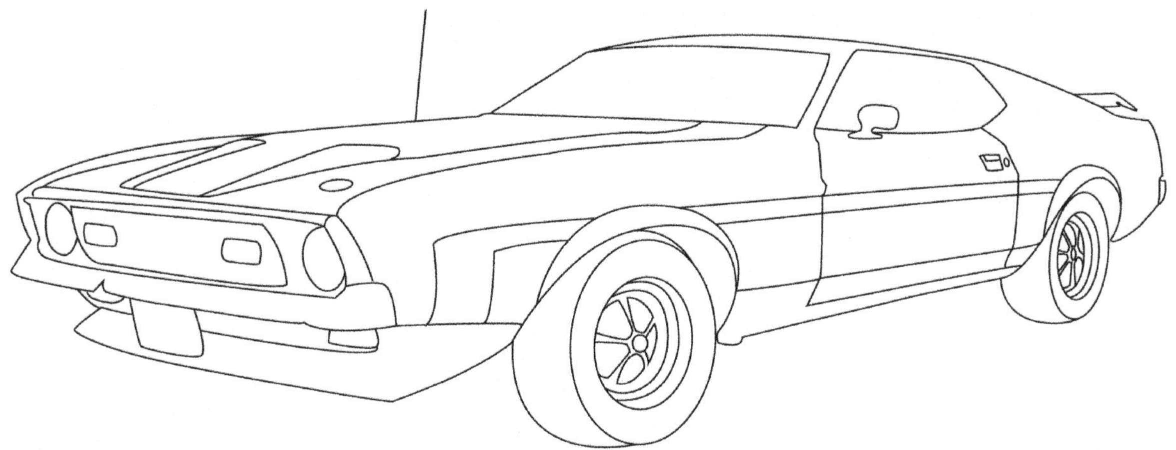

Lamborghini Veneno

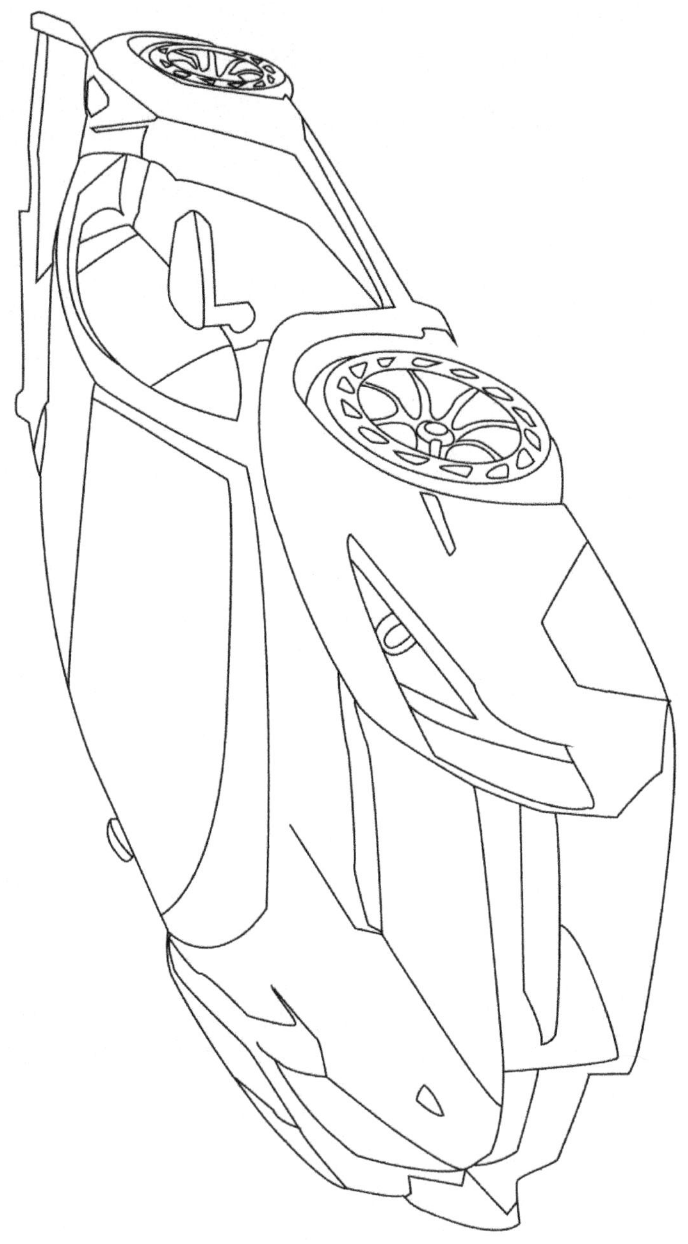

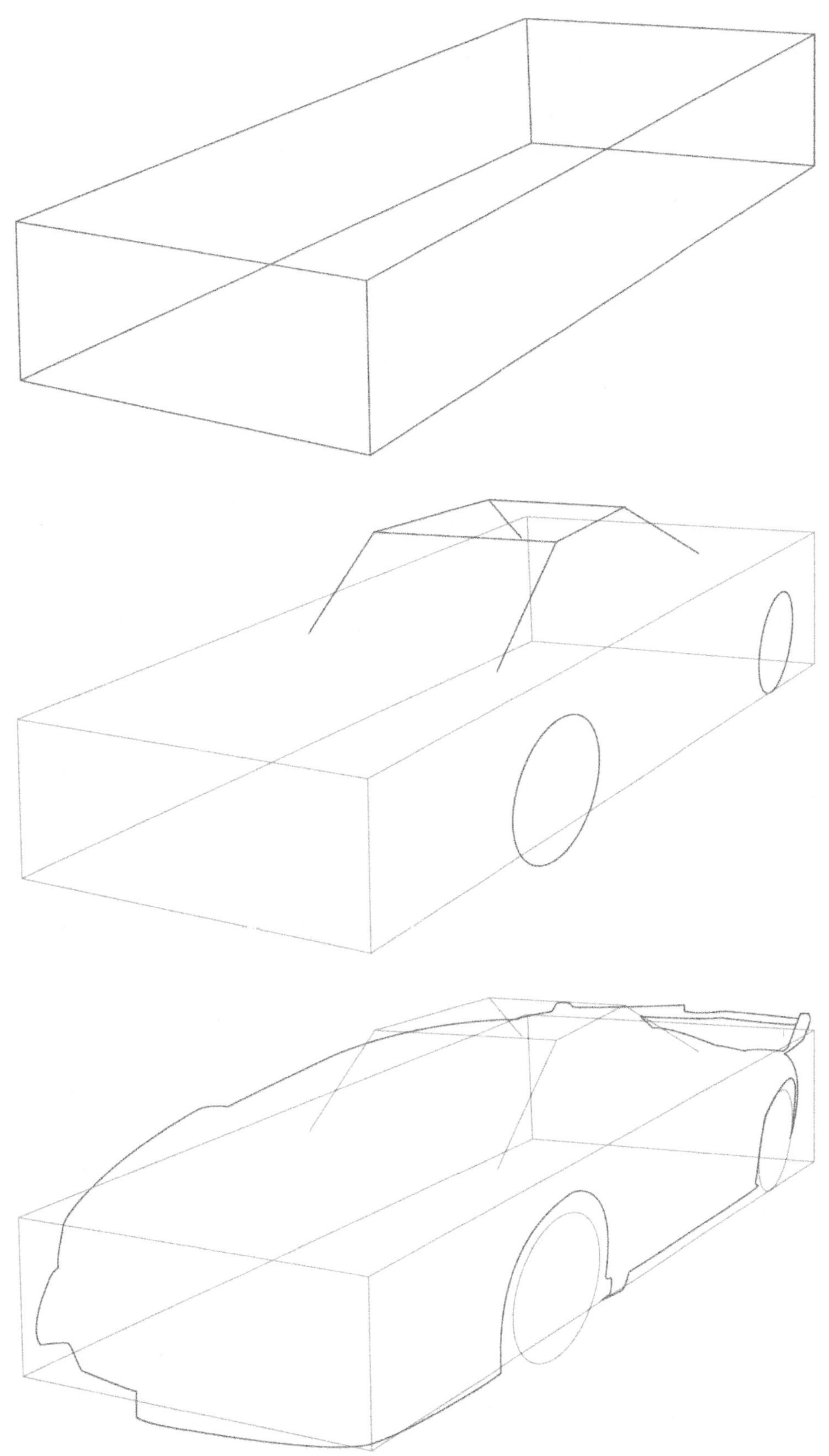

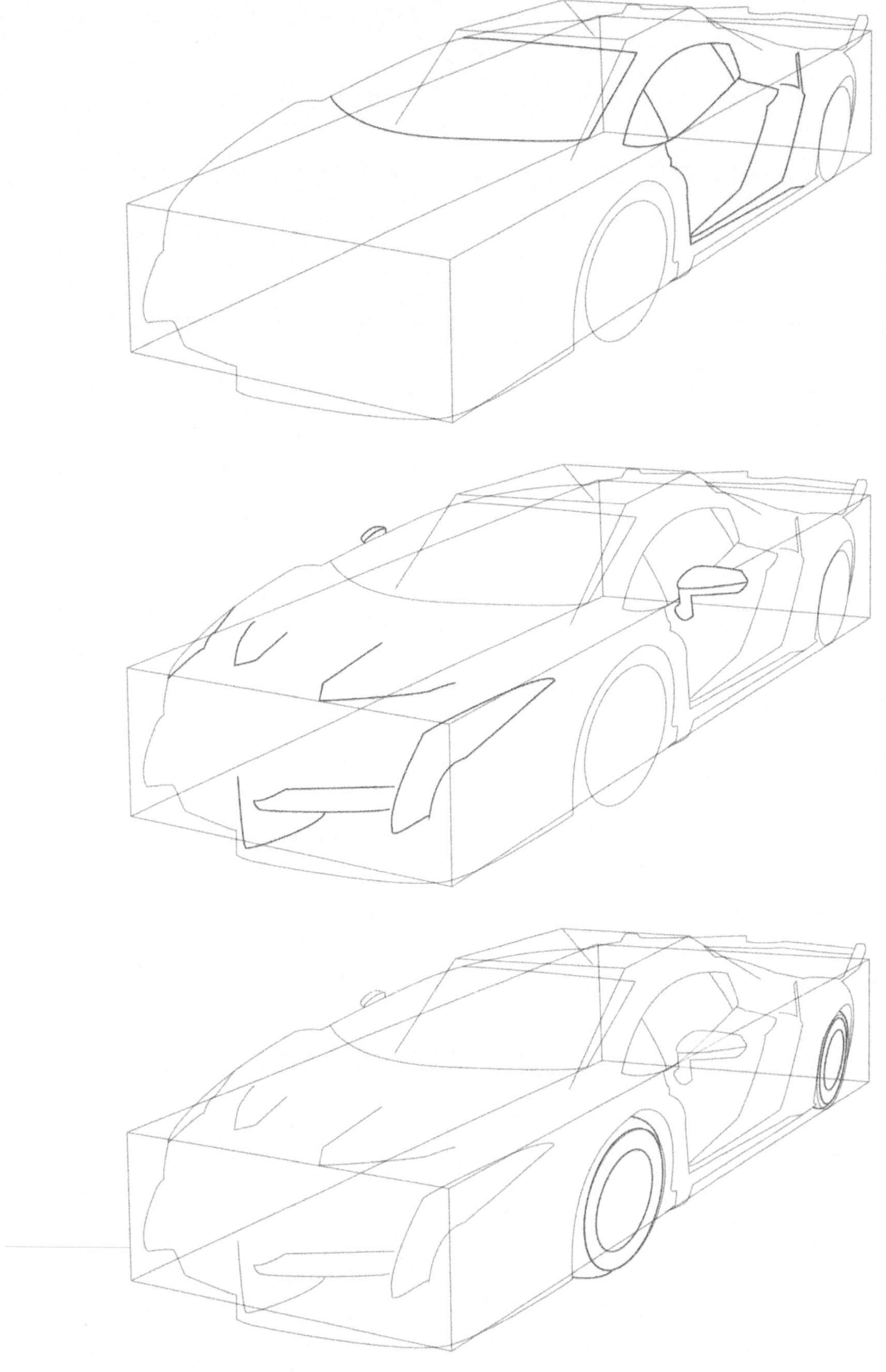

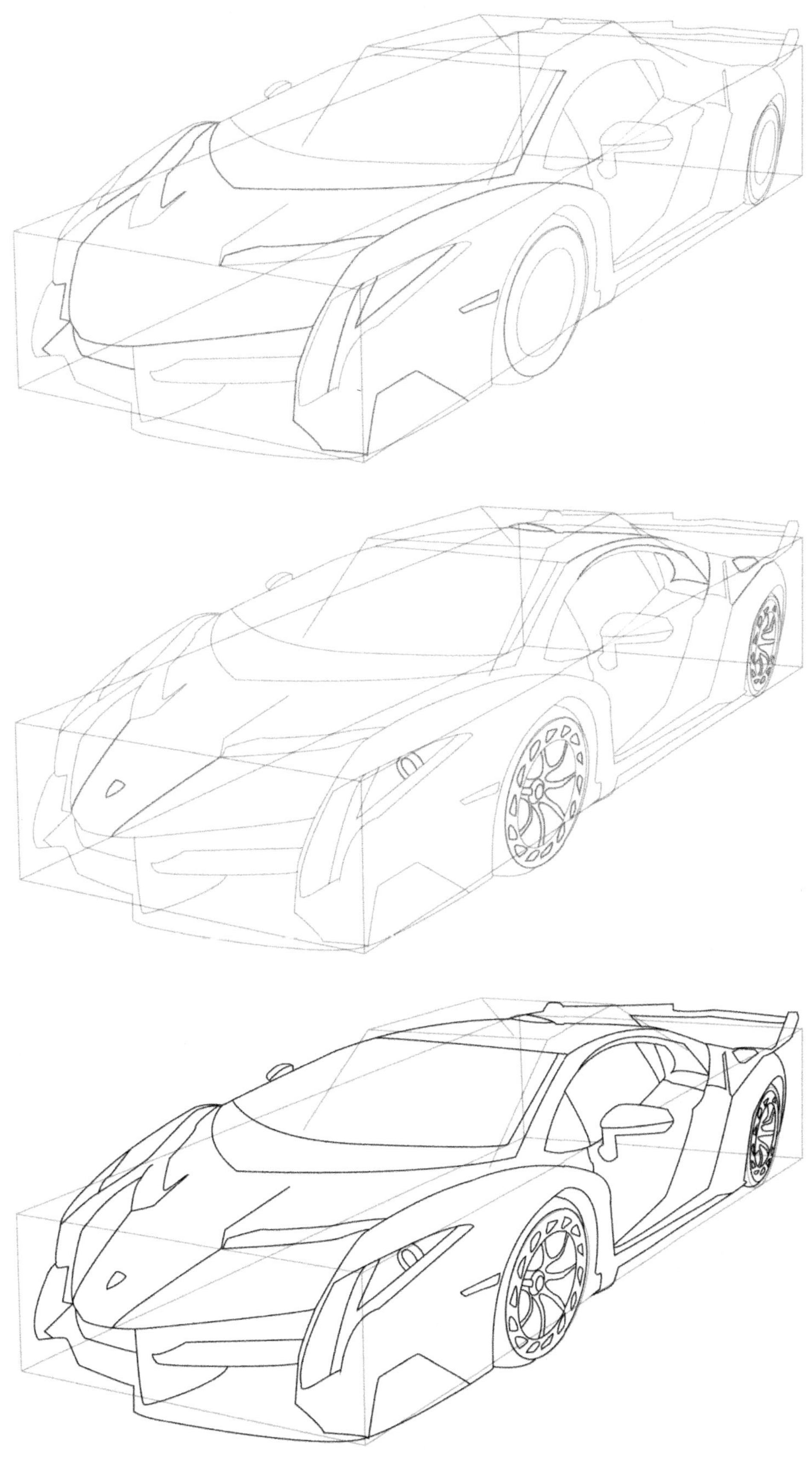

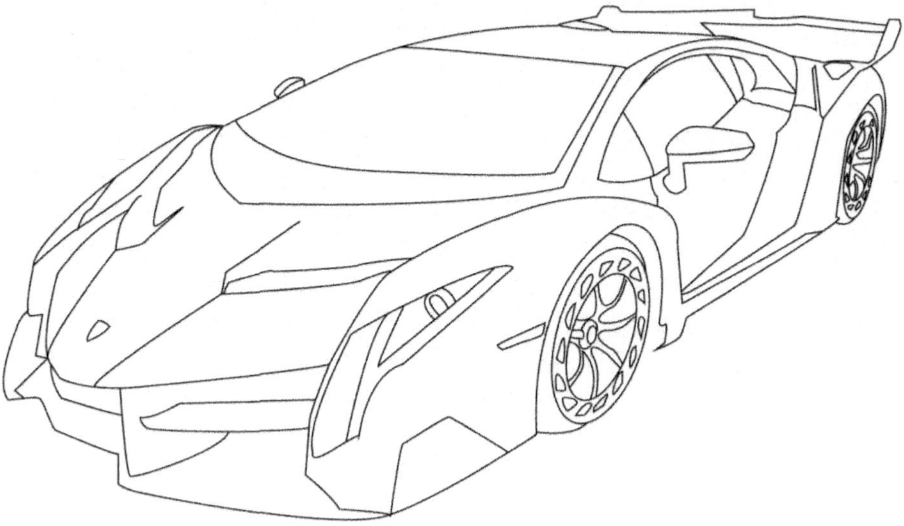

Ford Mustang Shelby GT500

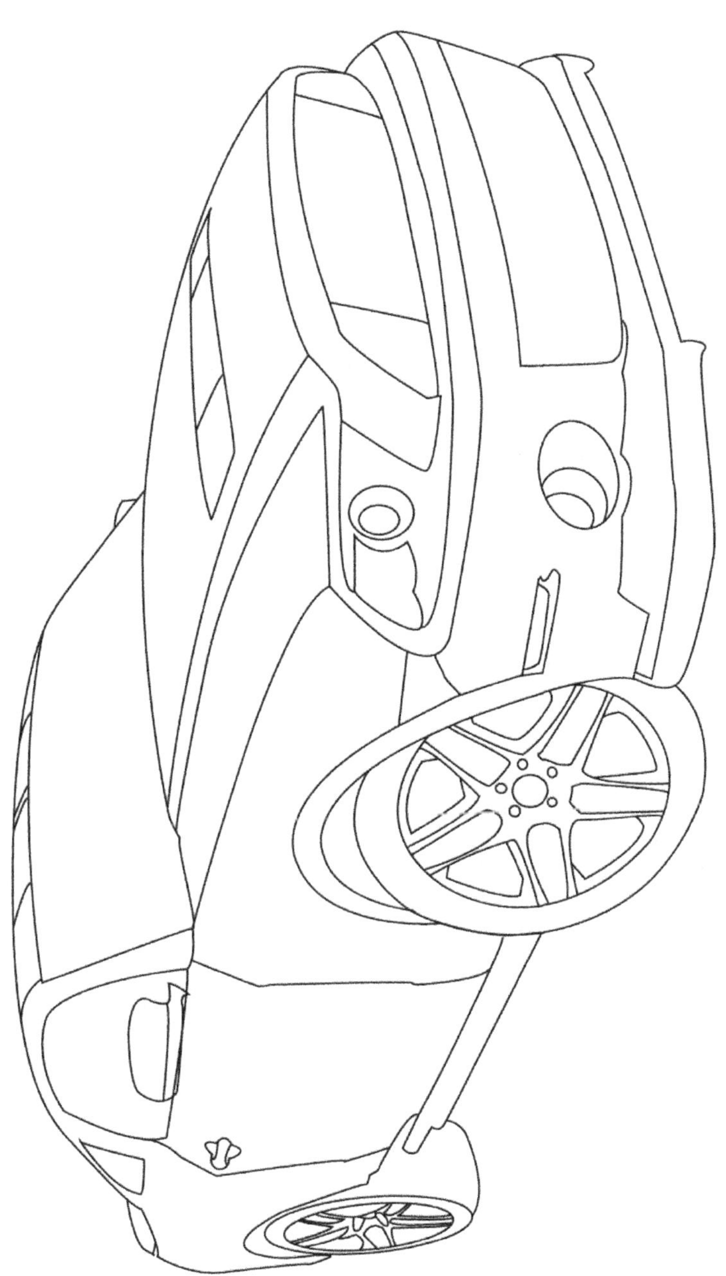

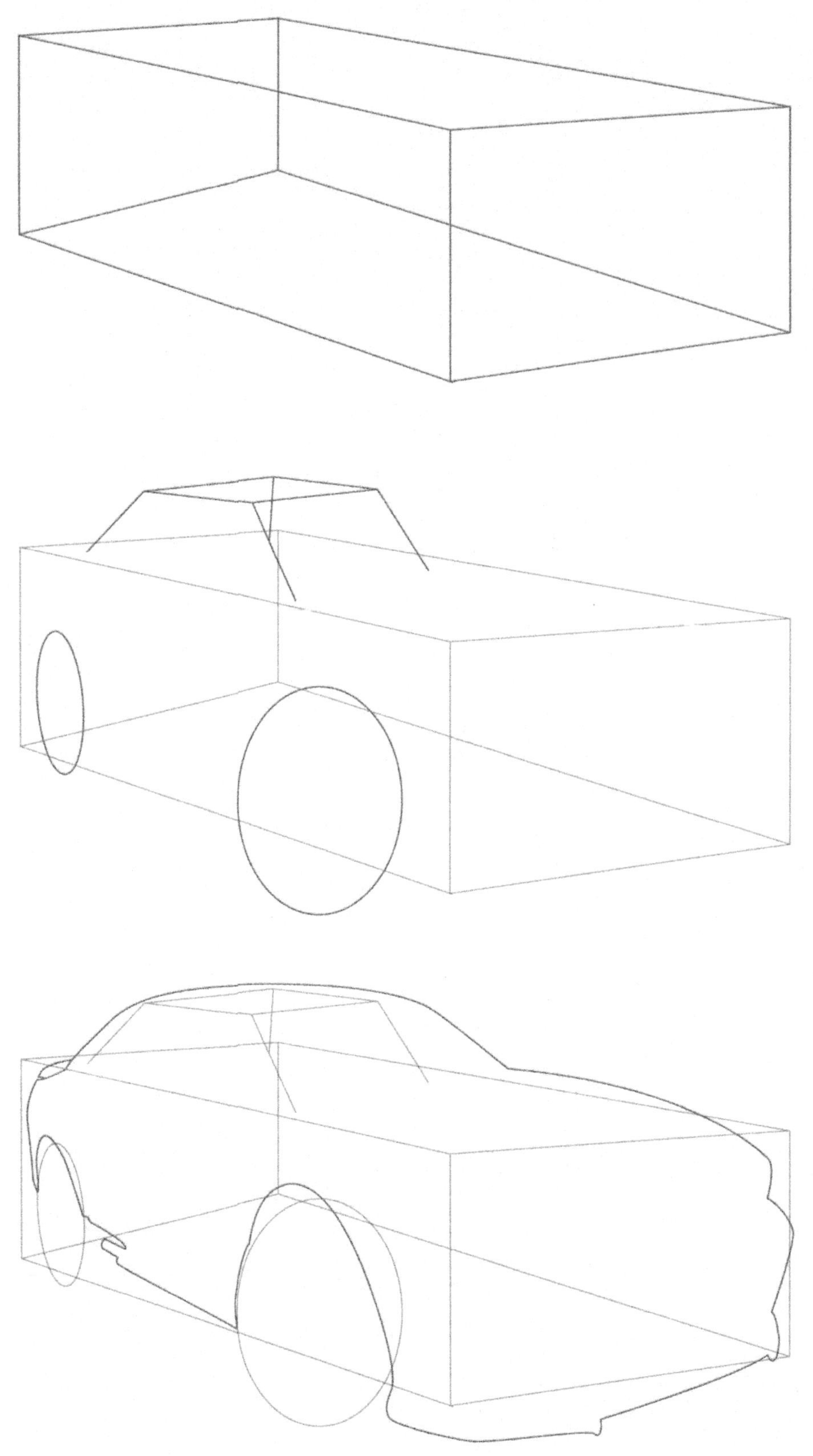

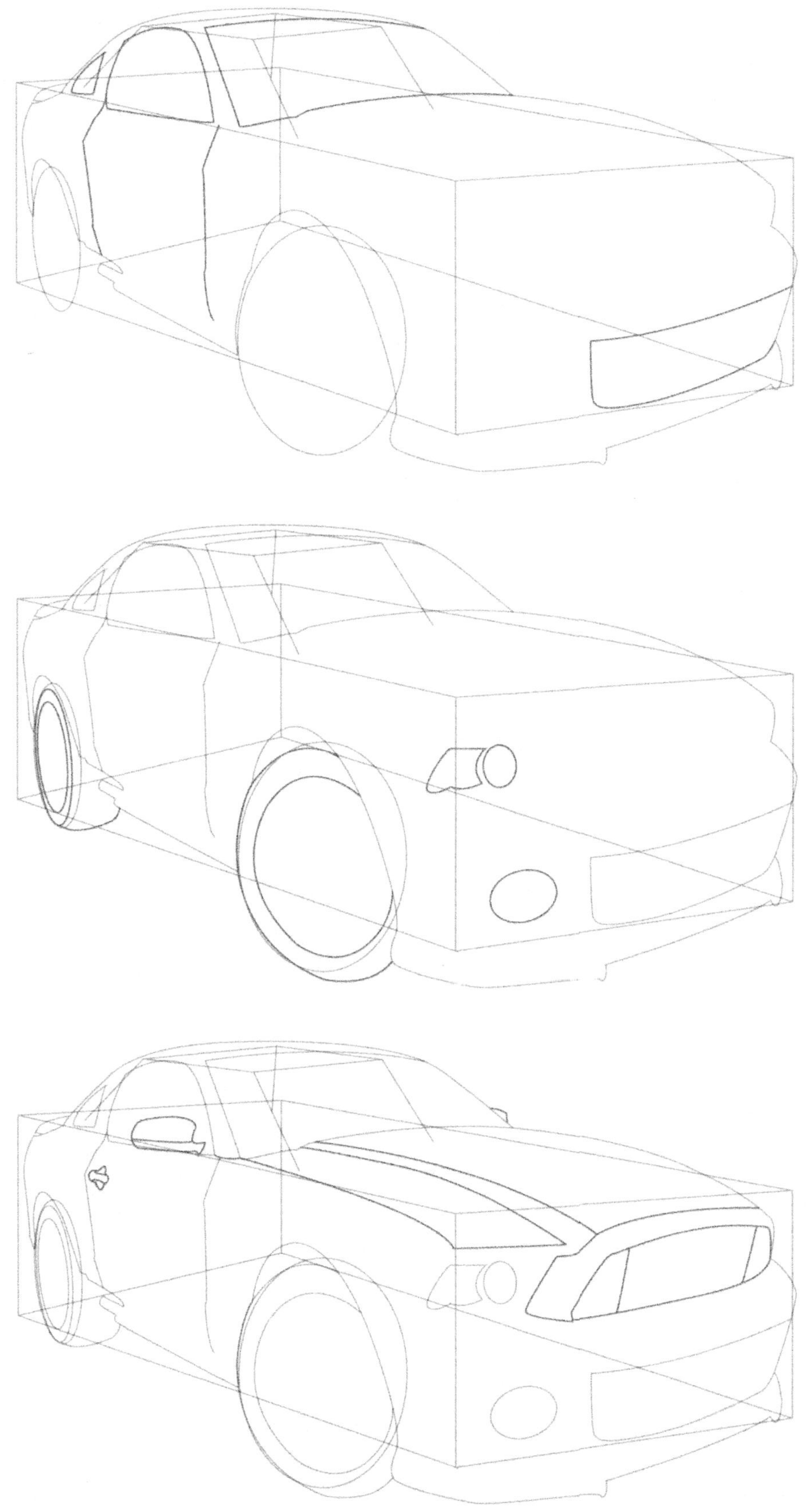

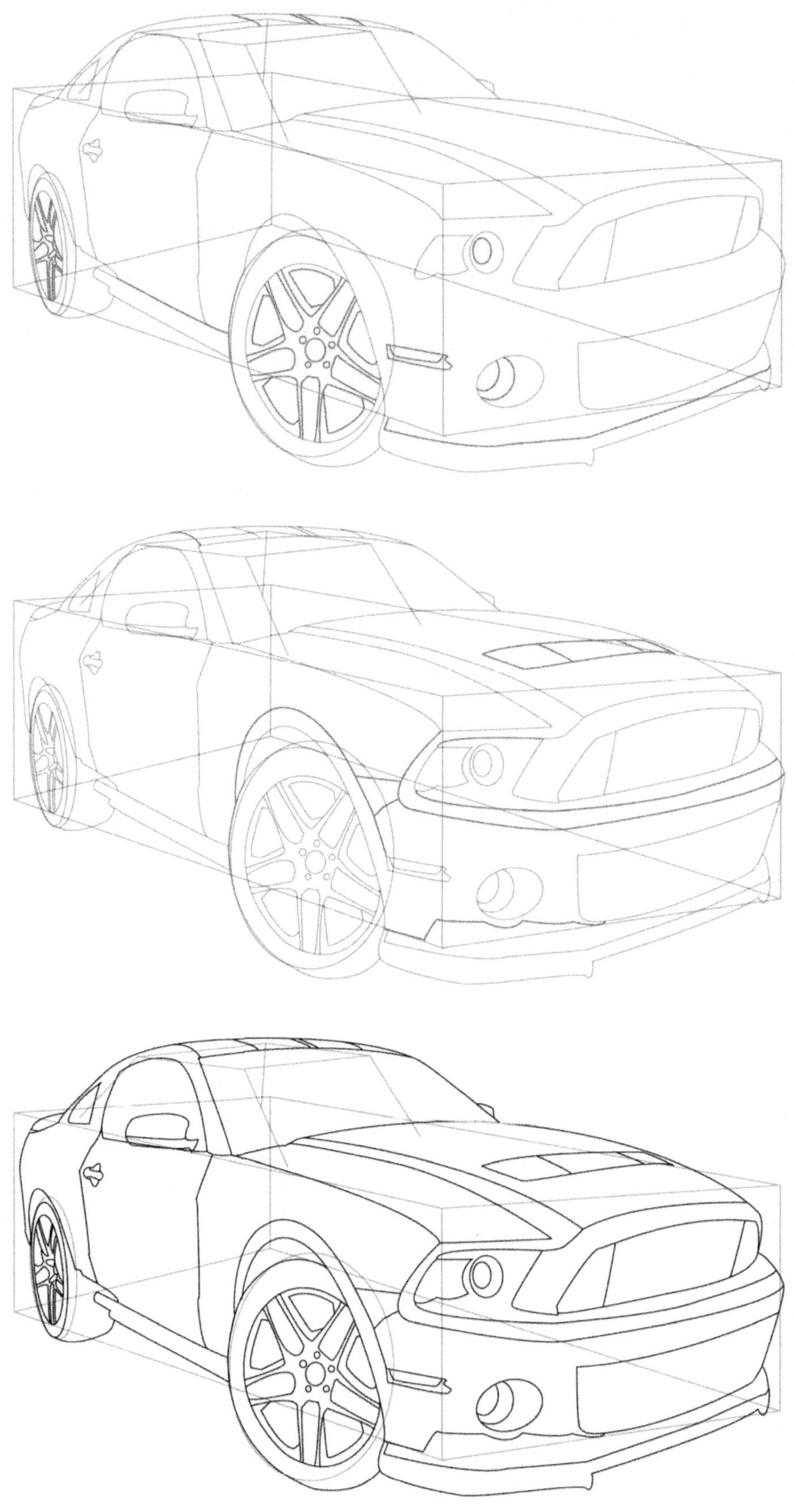

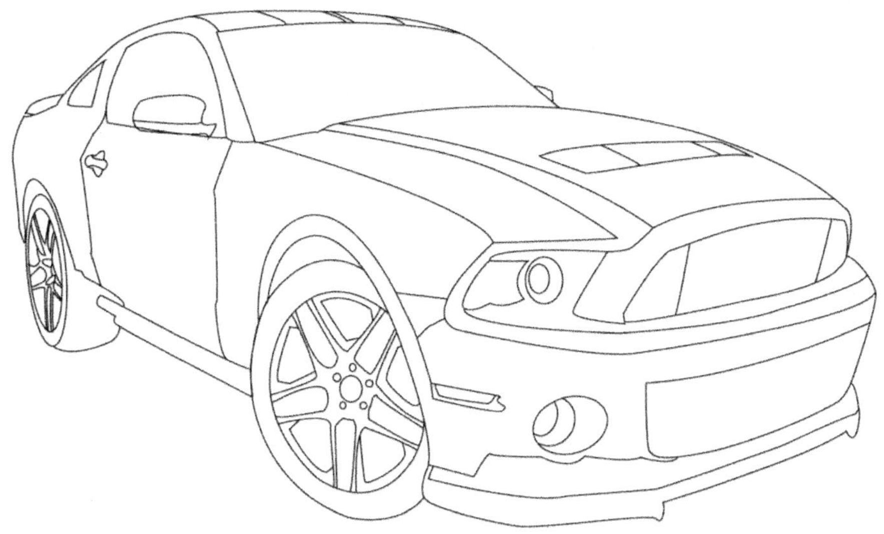

Chevrolet Corvette Grand Sport C7

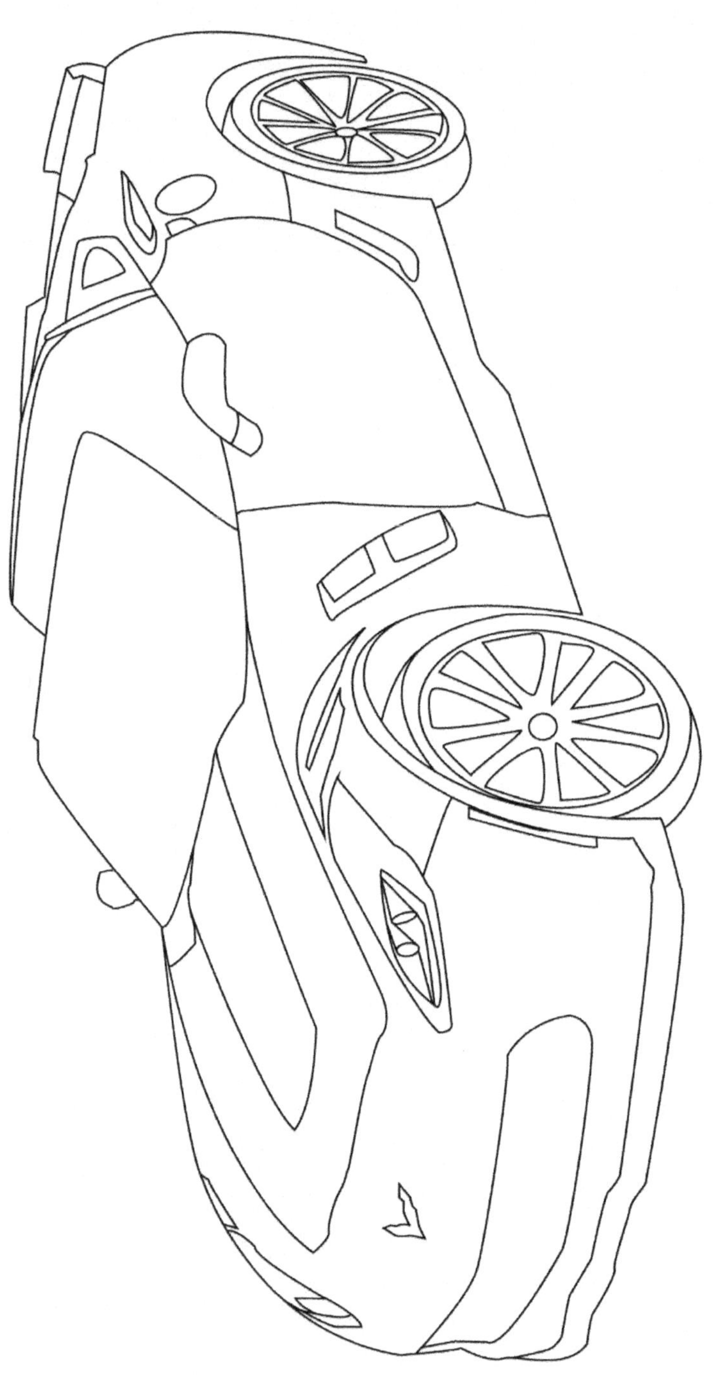

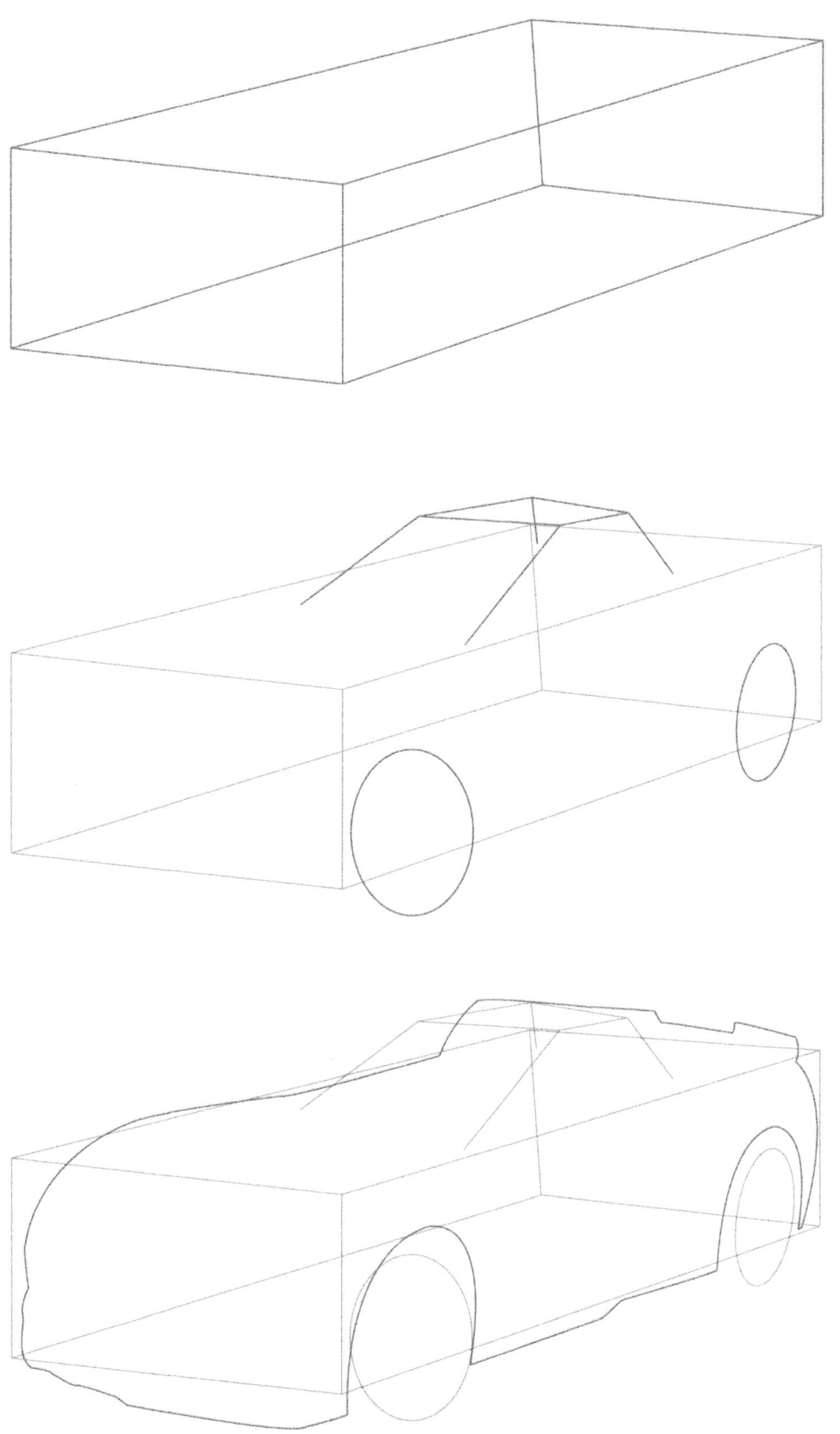

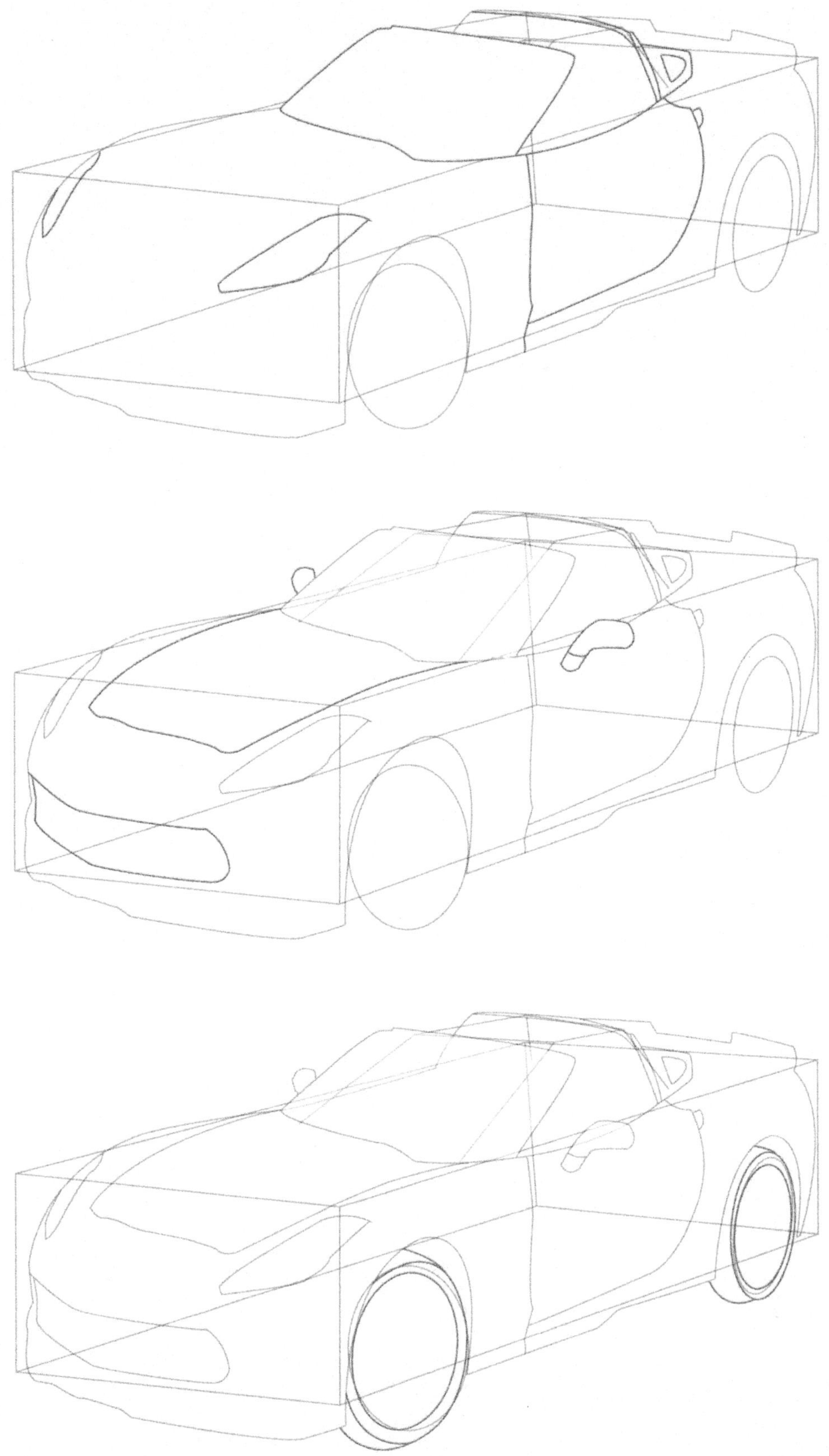

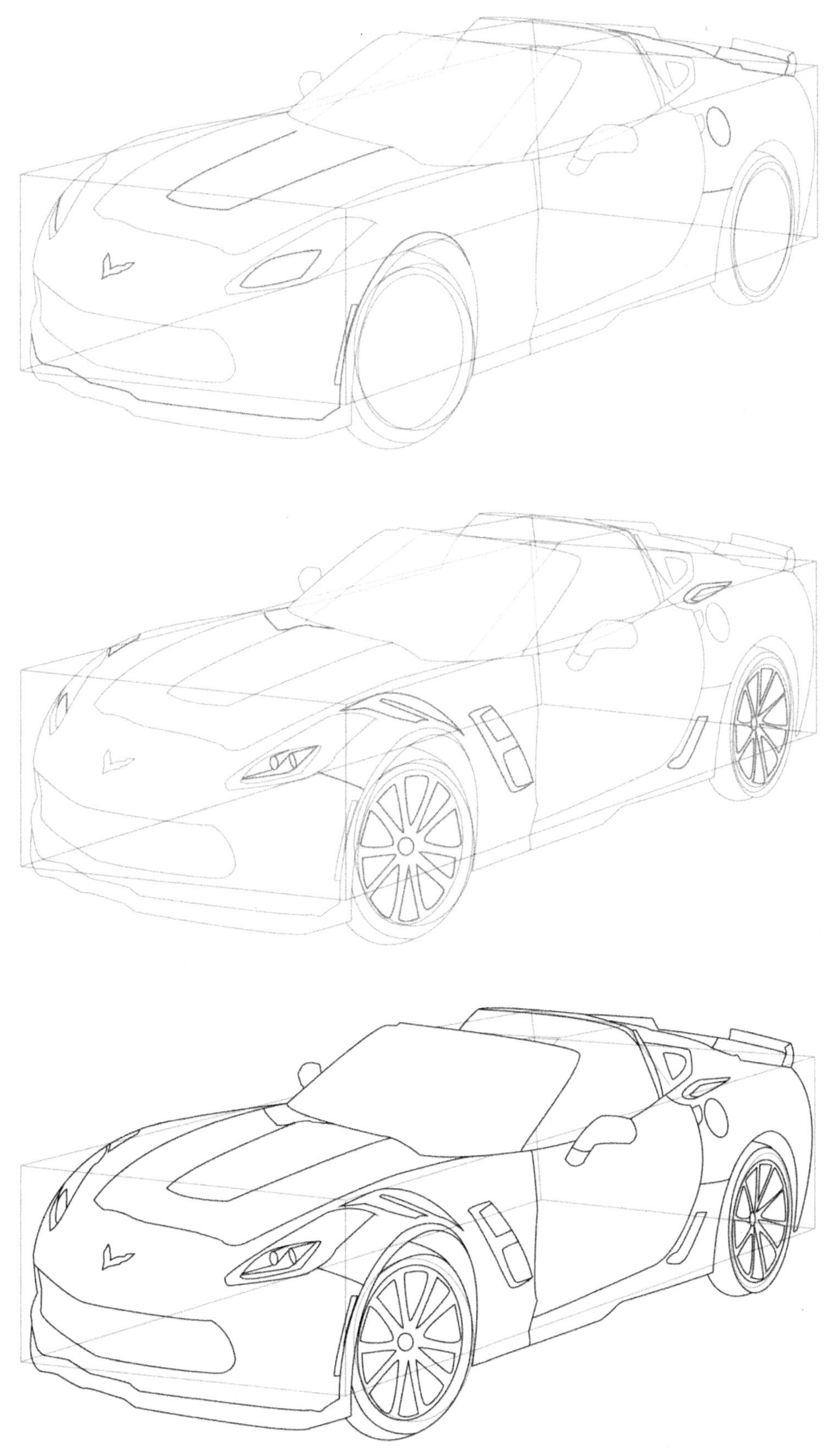

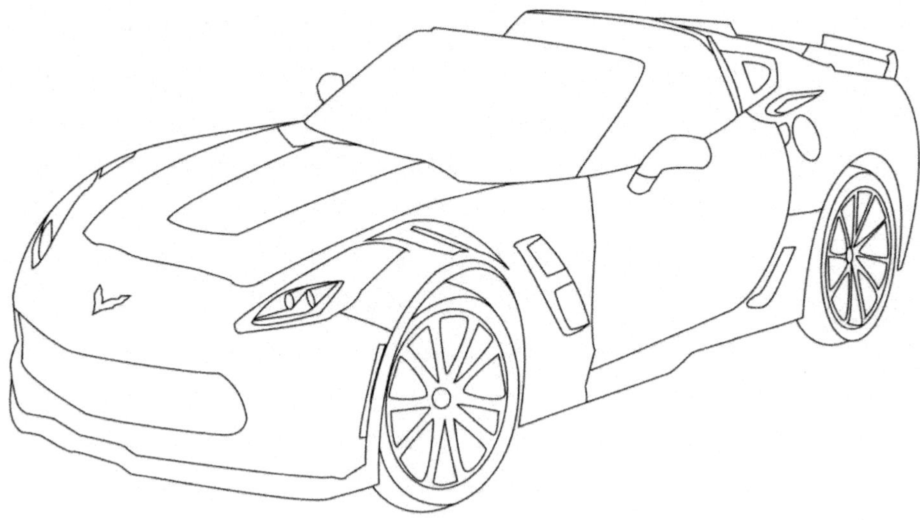

Dodge Viper GTS

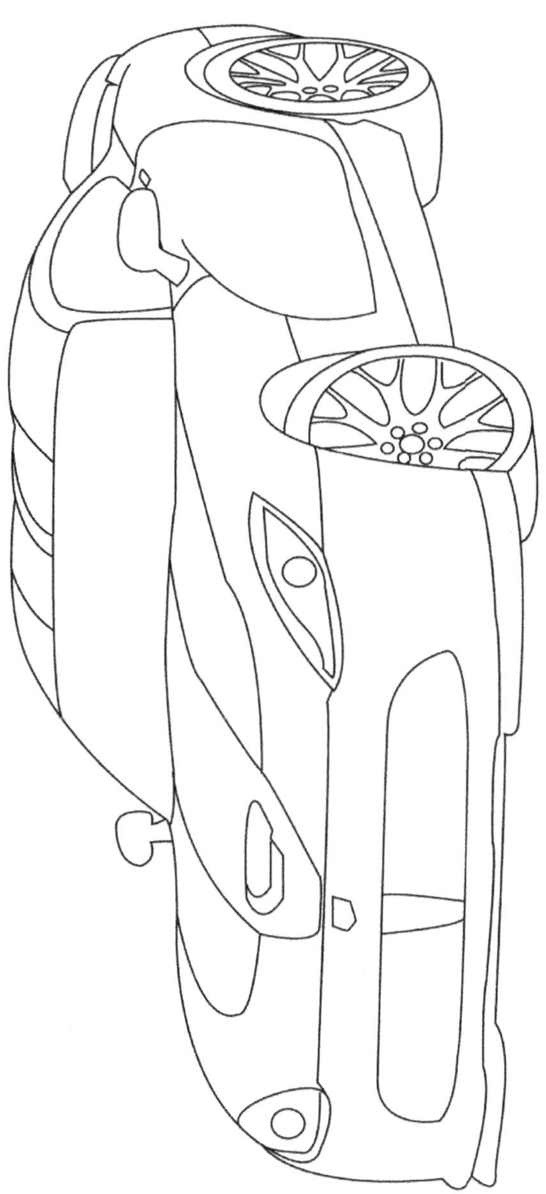

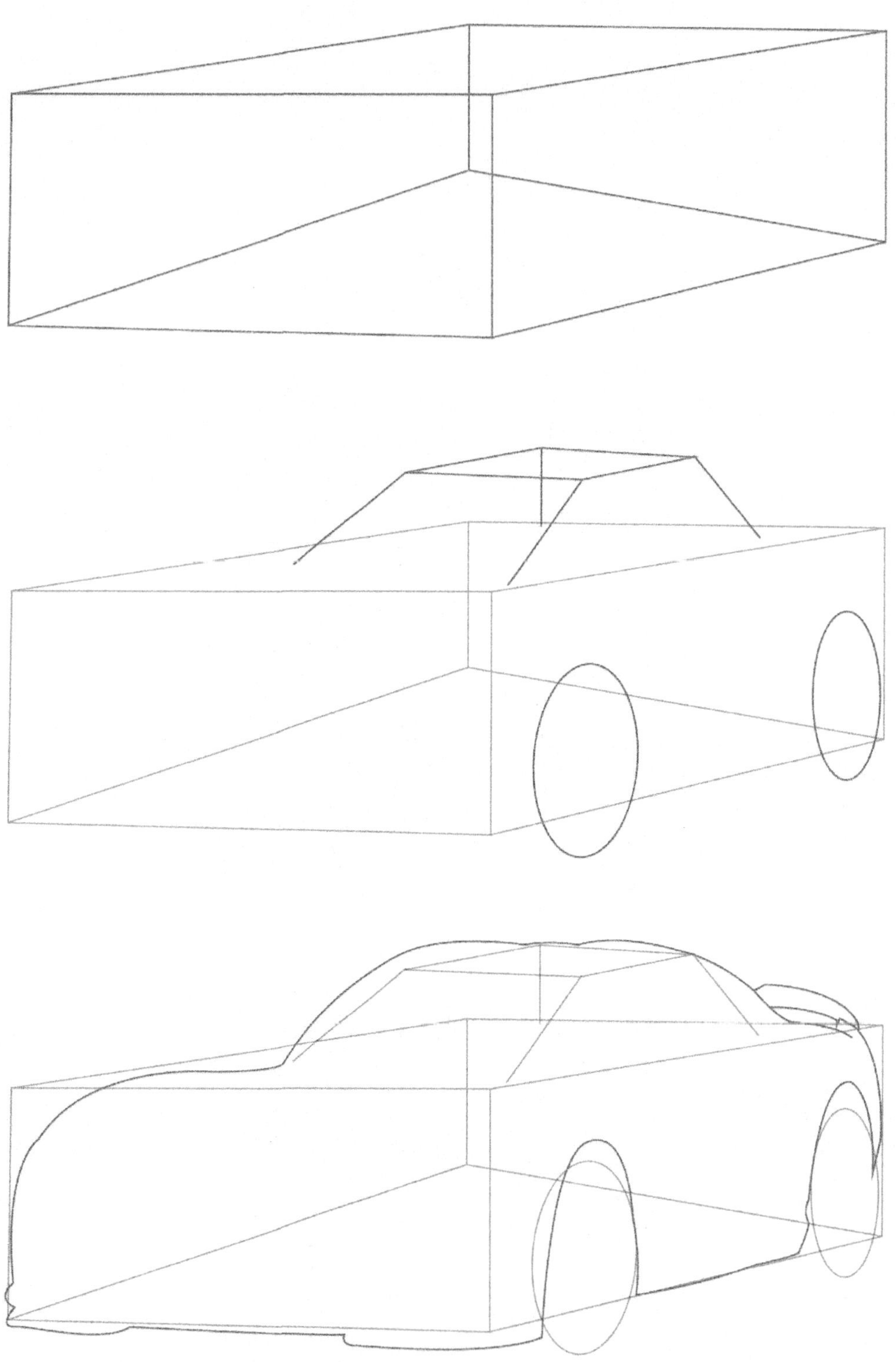

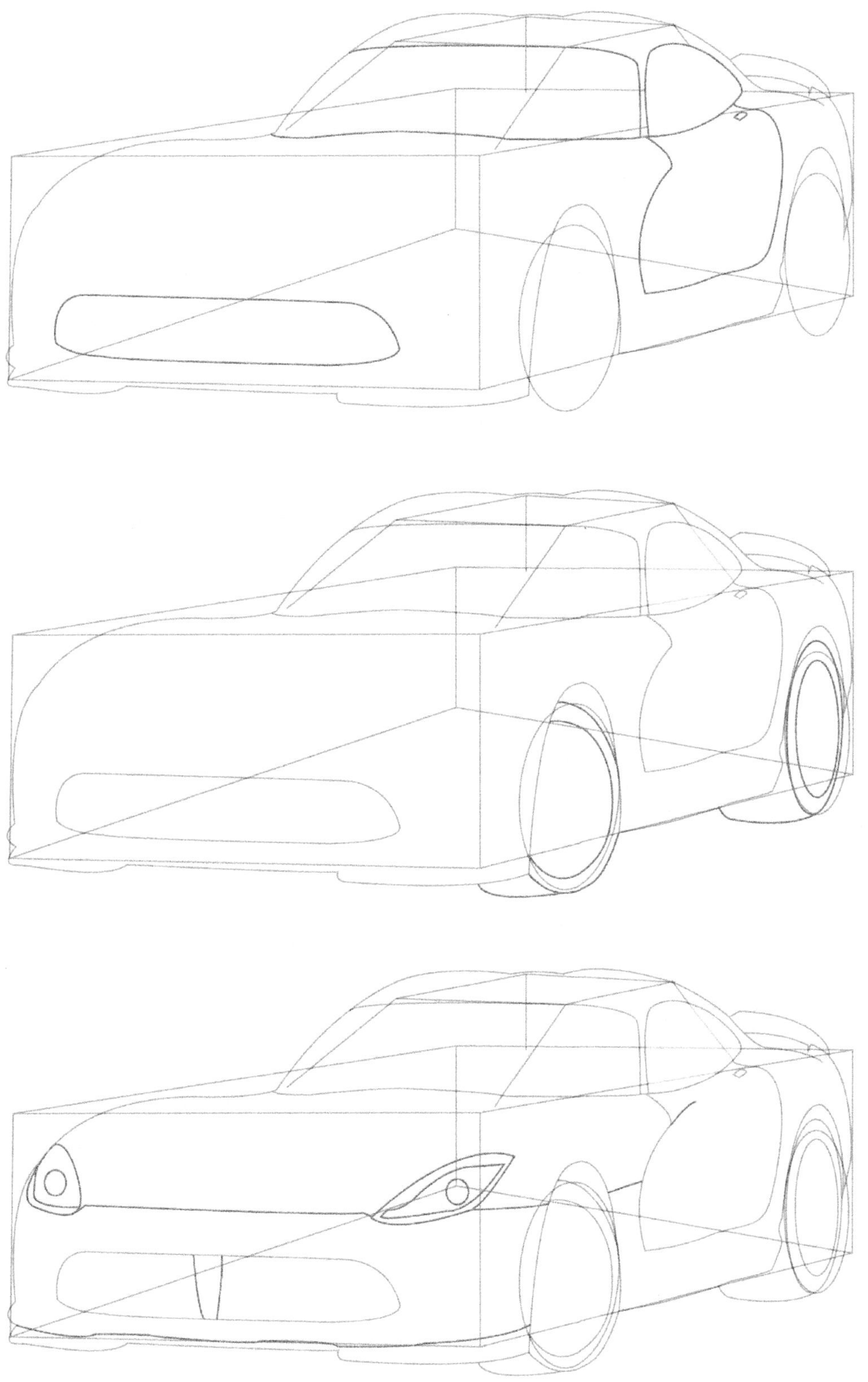

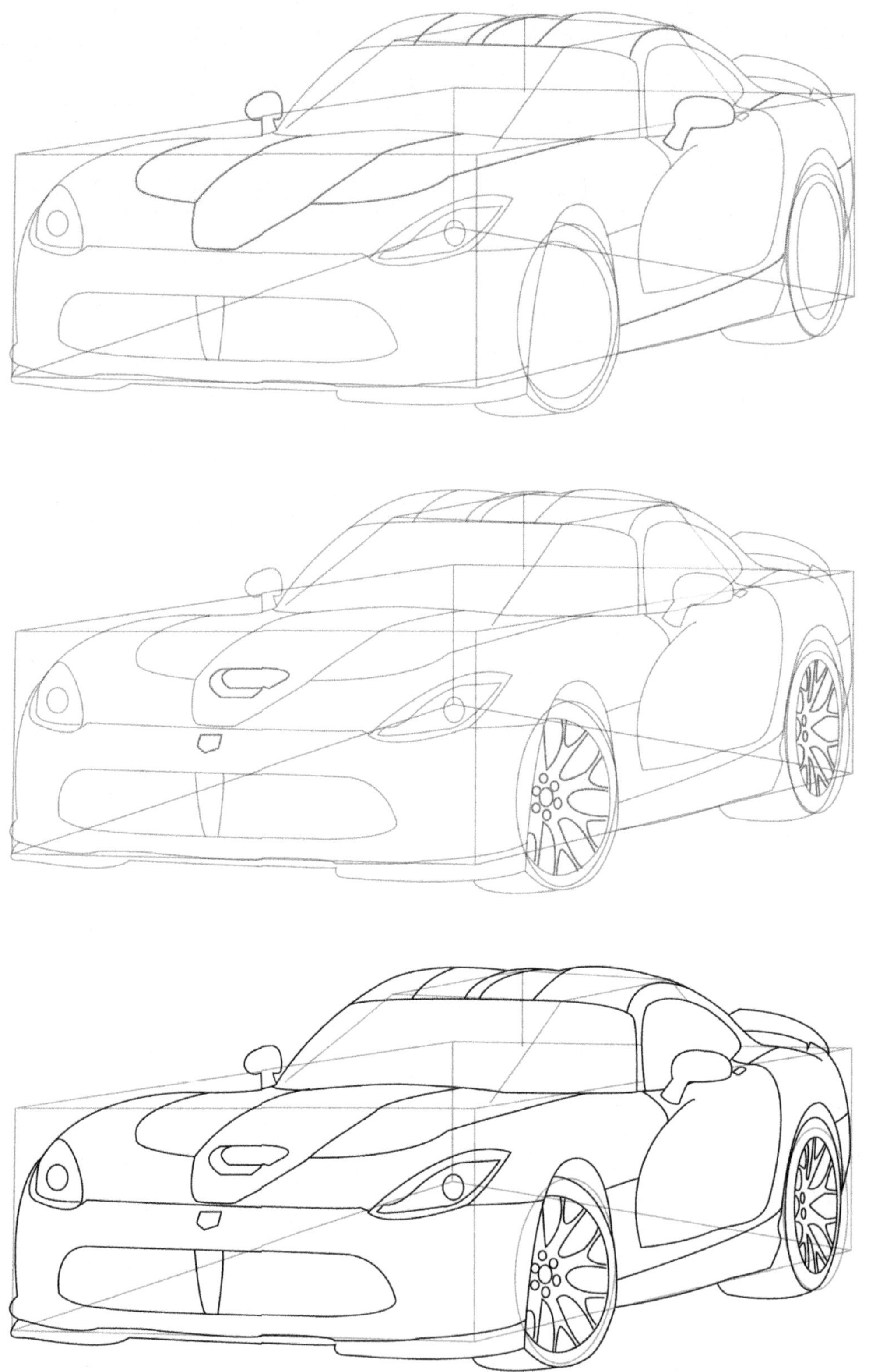

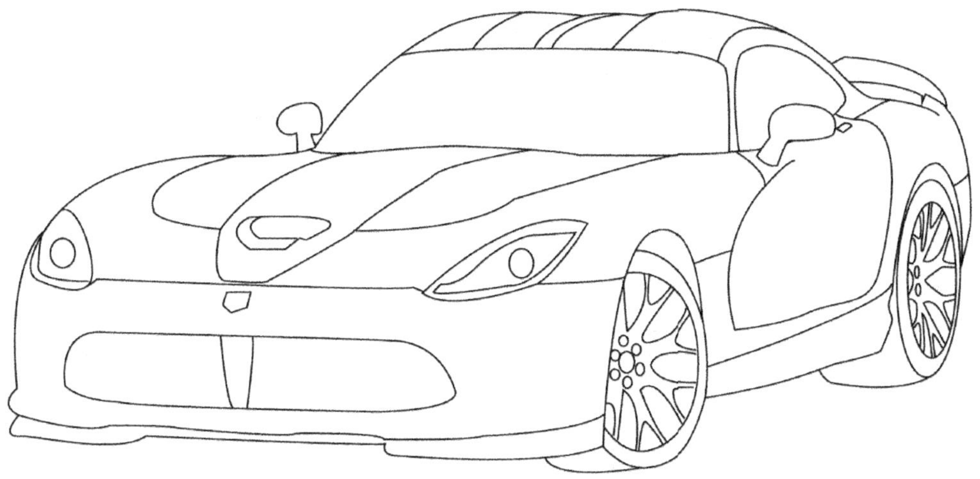

Lamborghini Gallardo

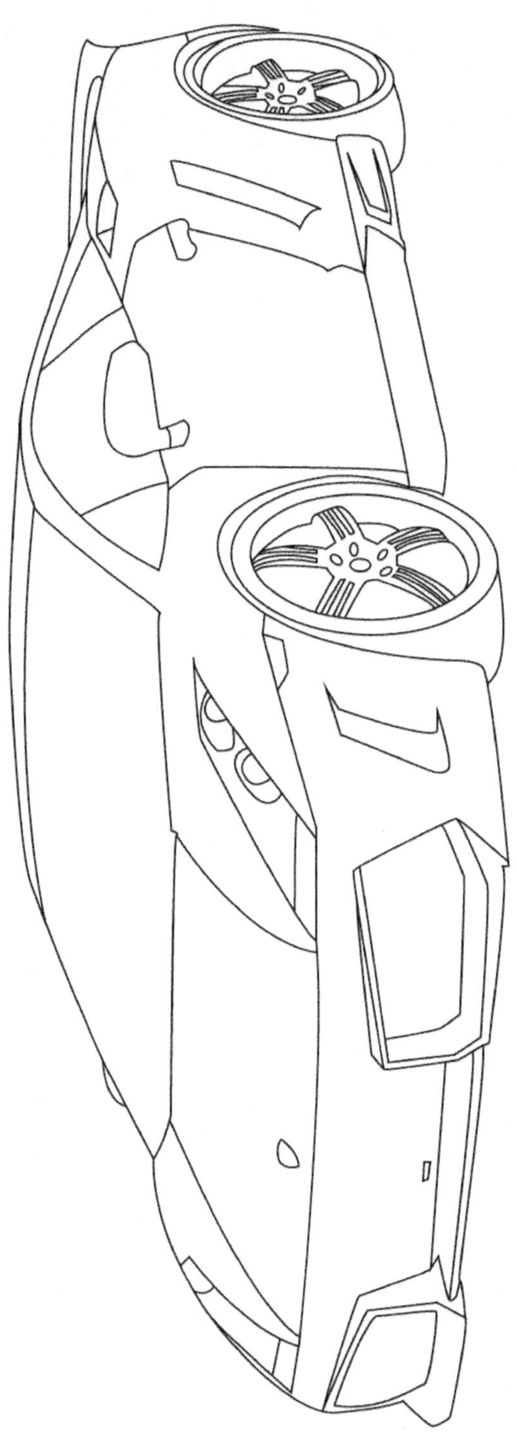

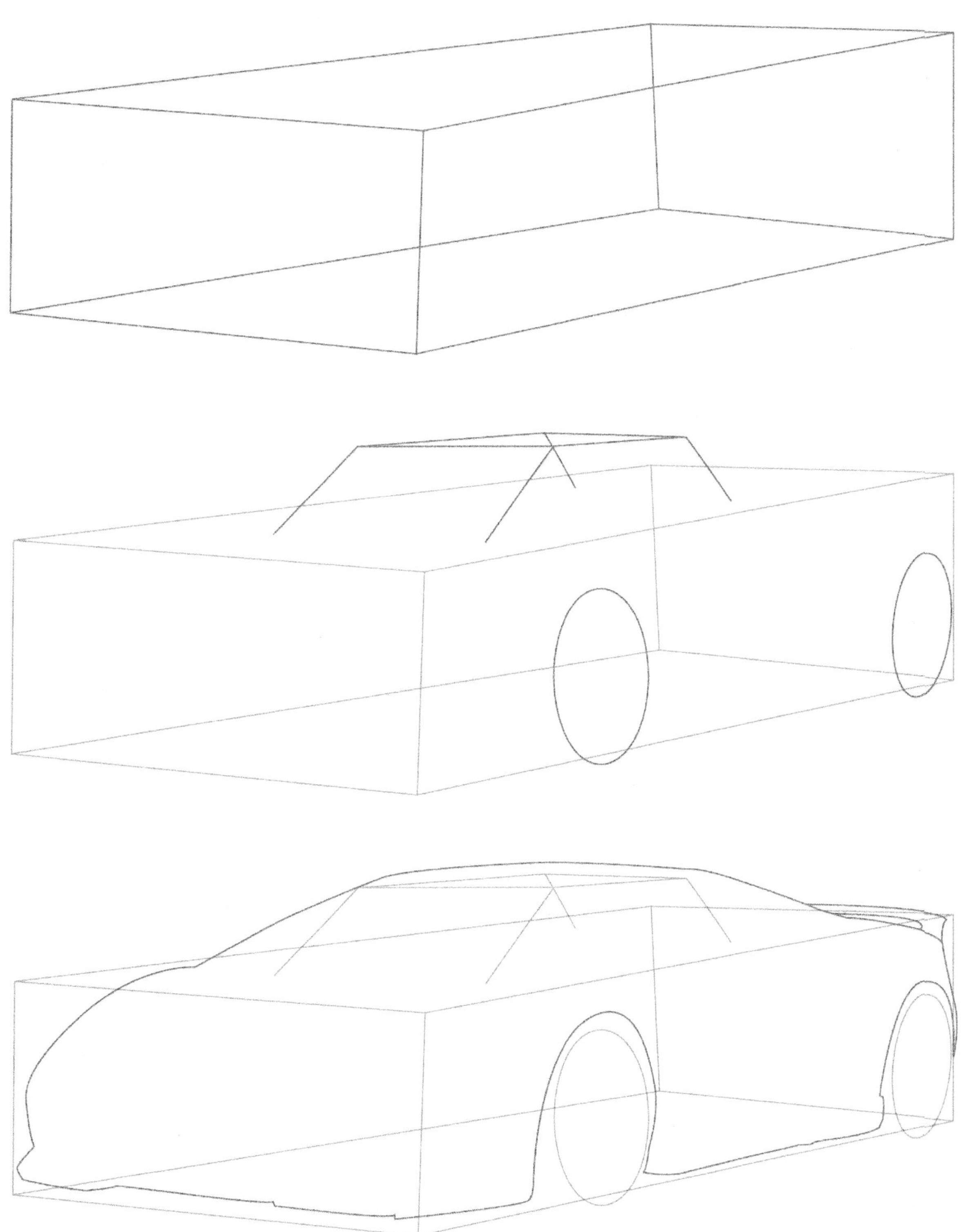

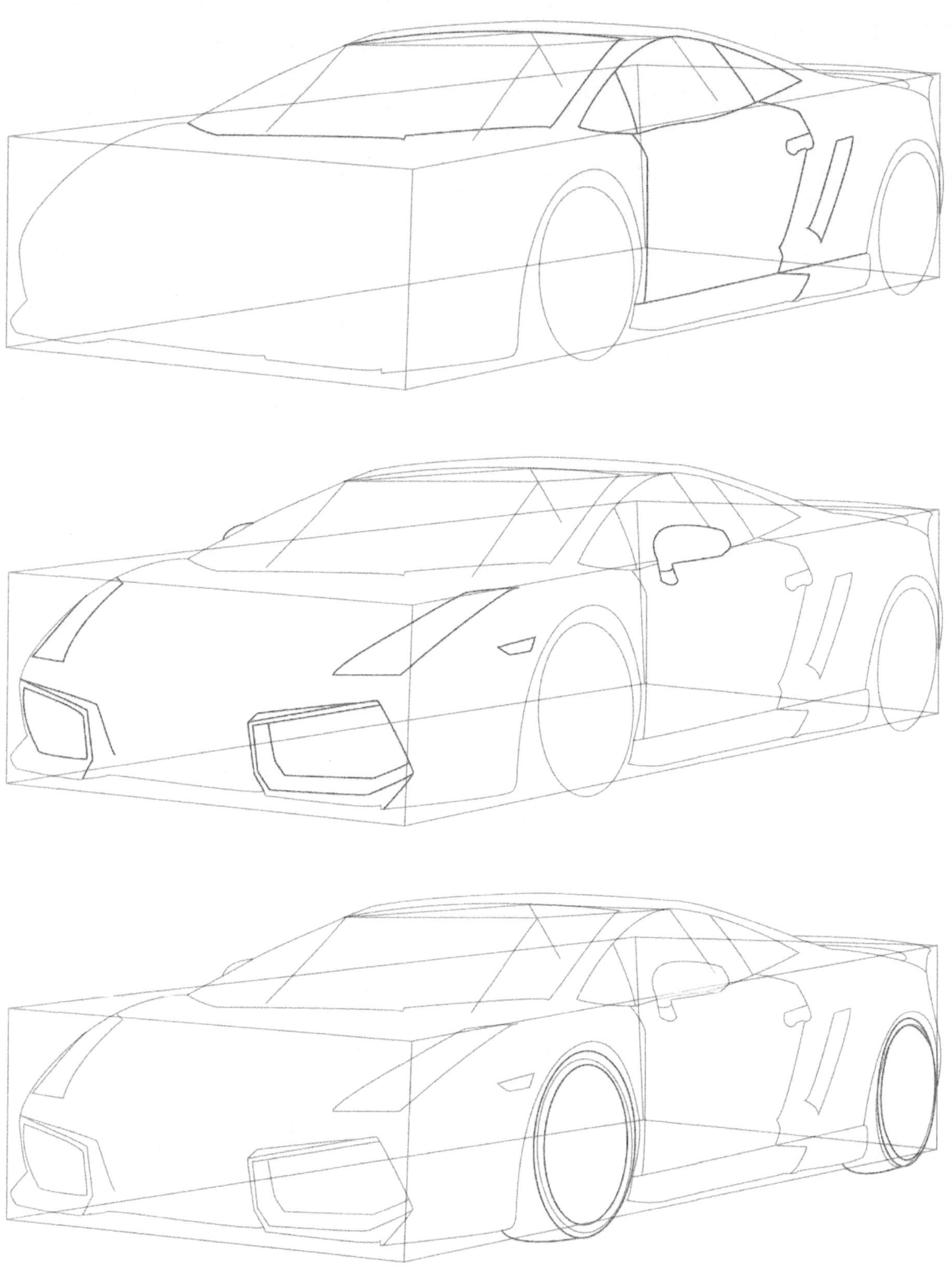

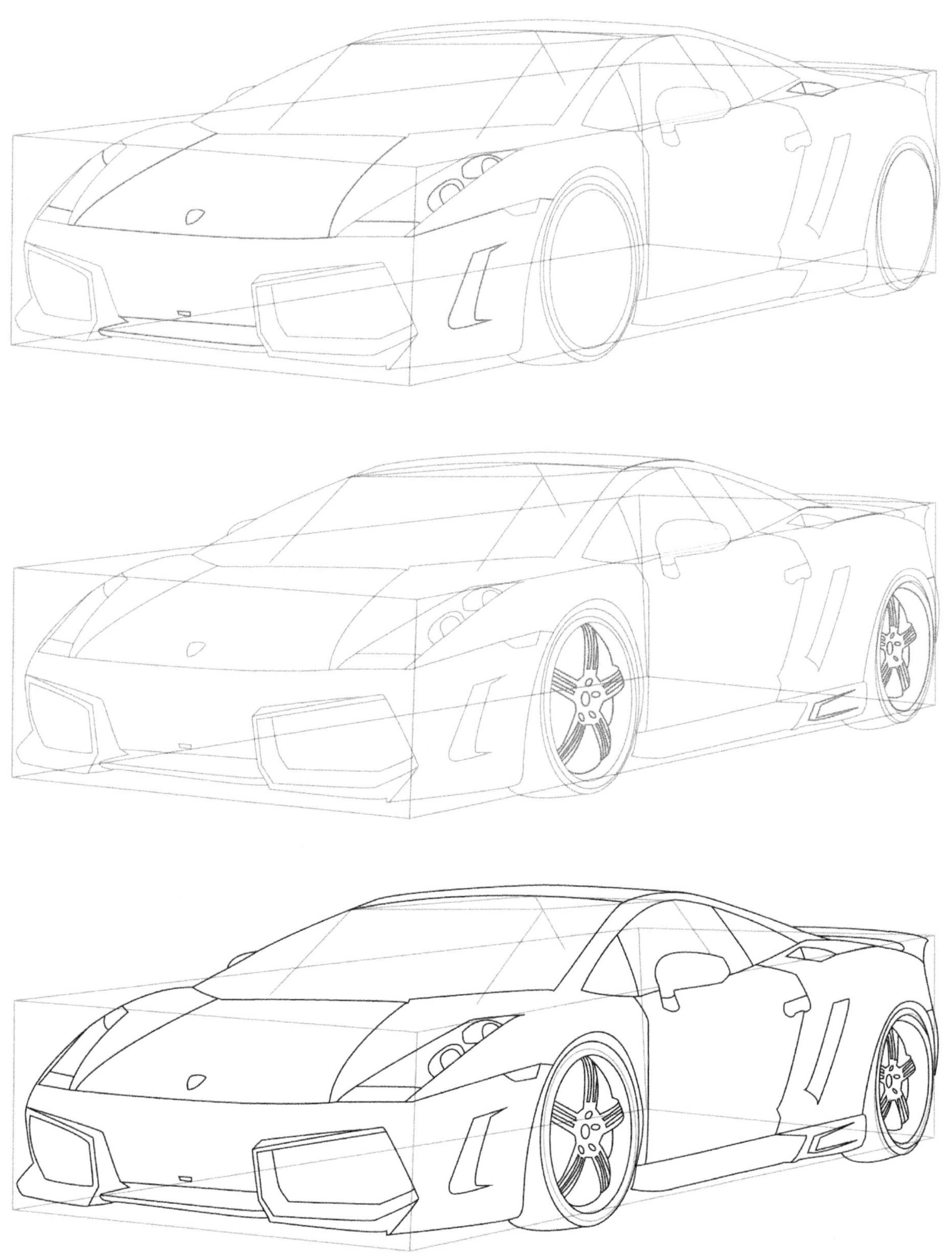

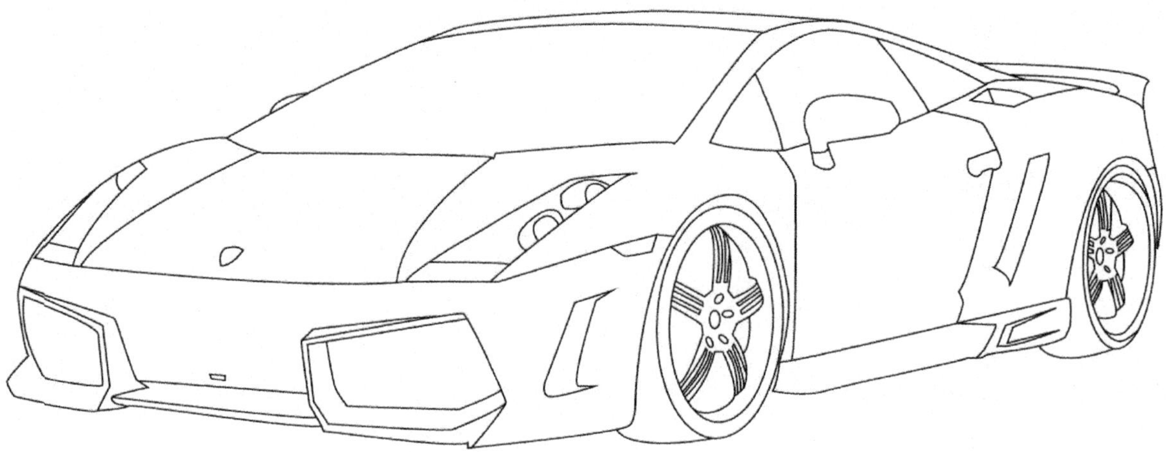

Bugatti Divo

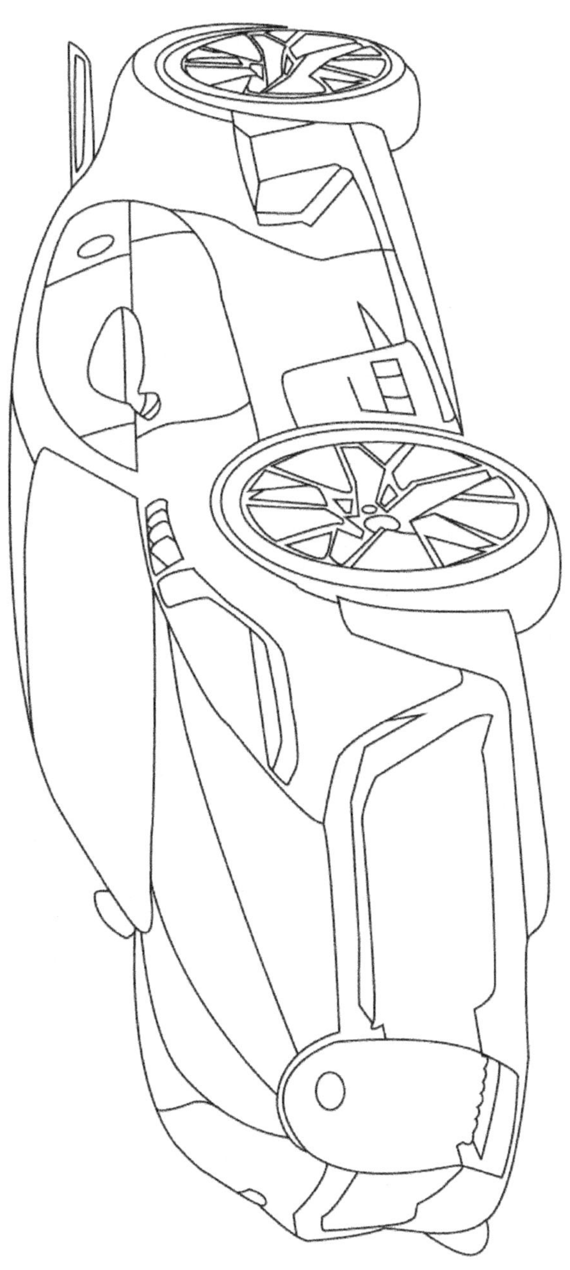

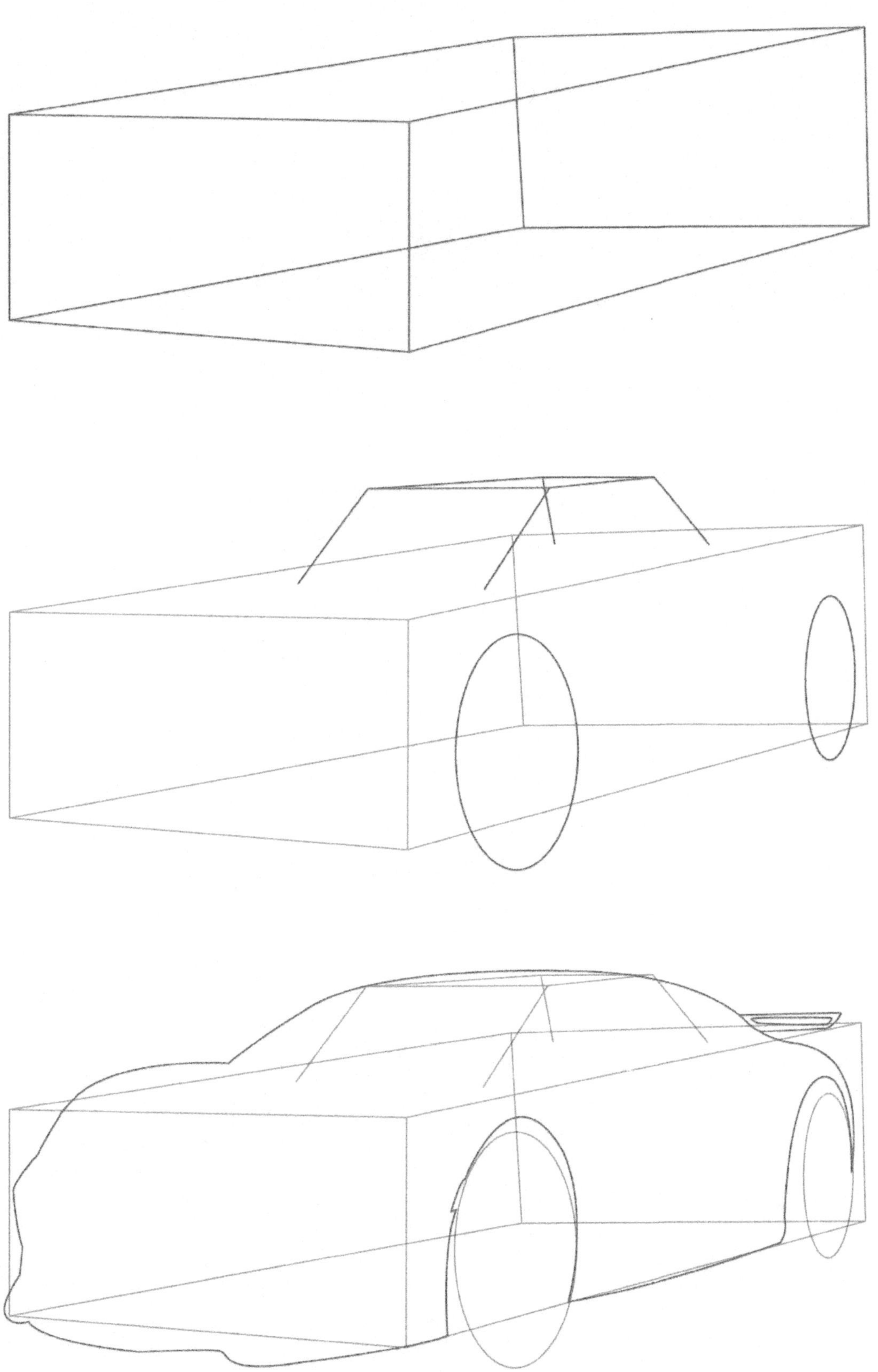

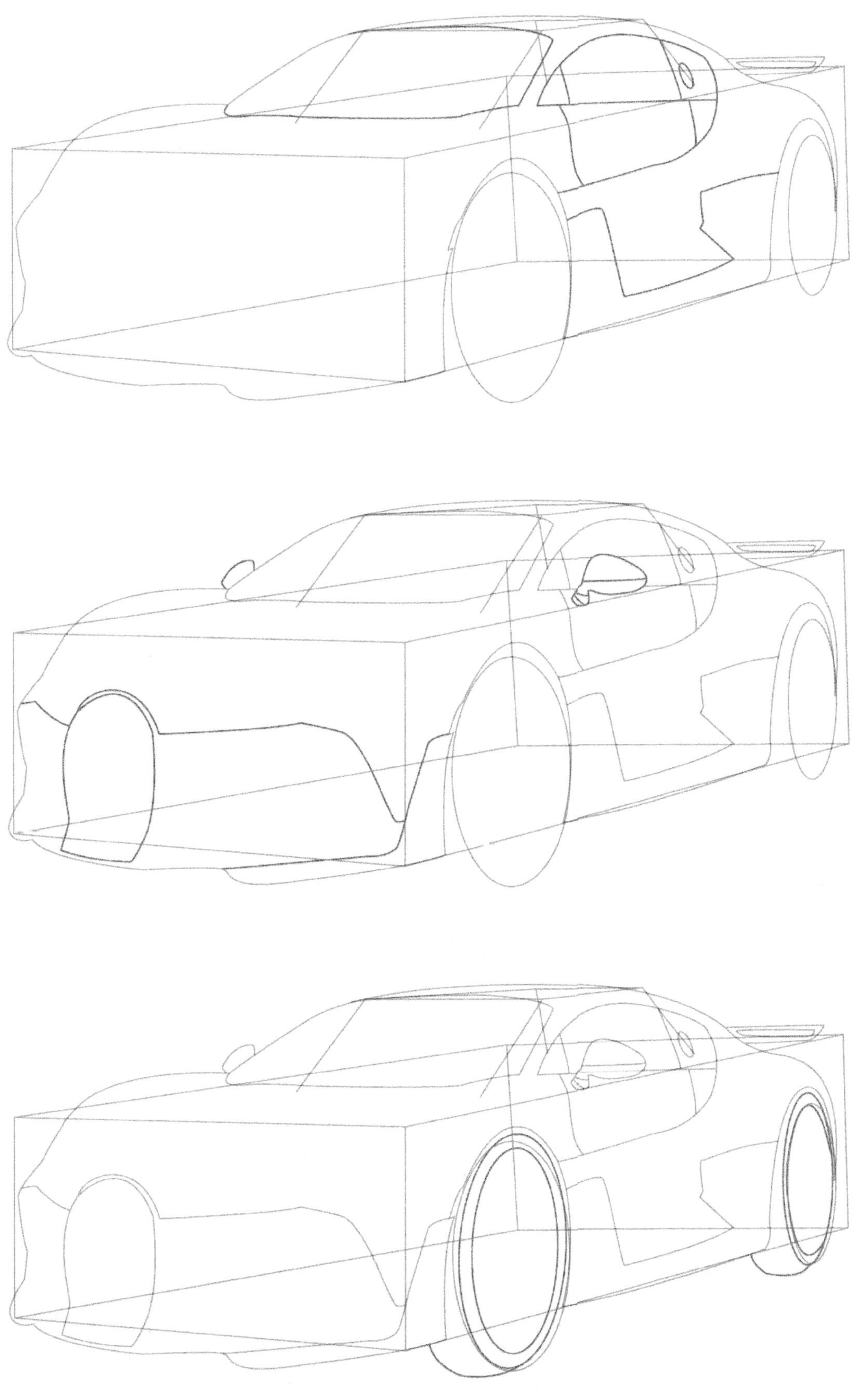

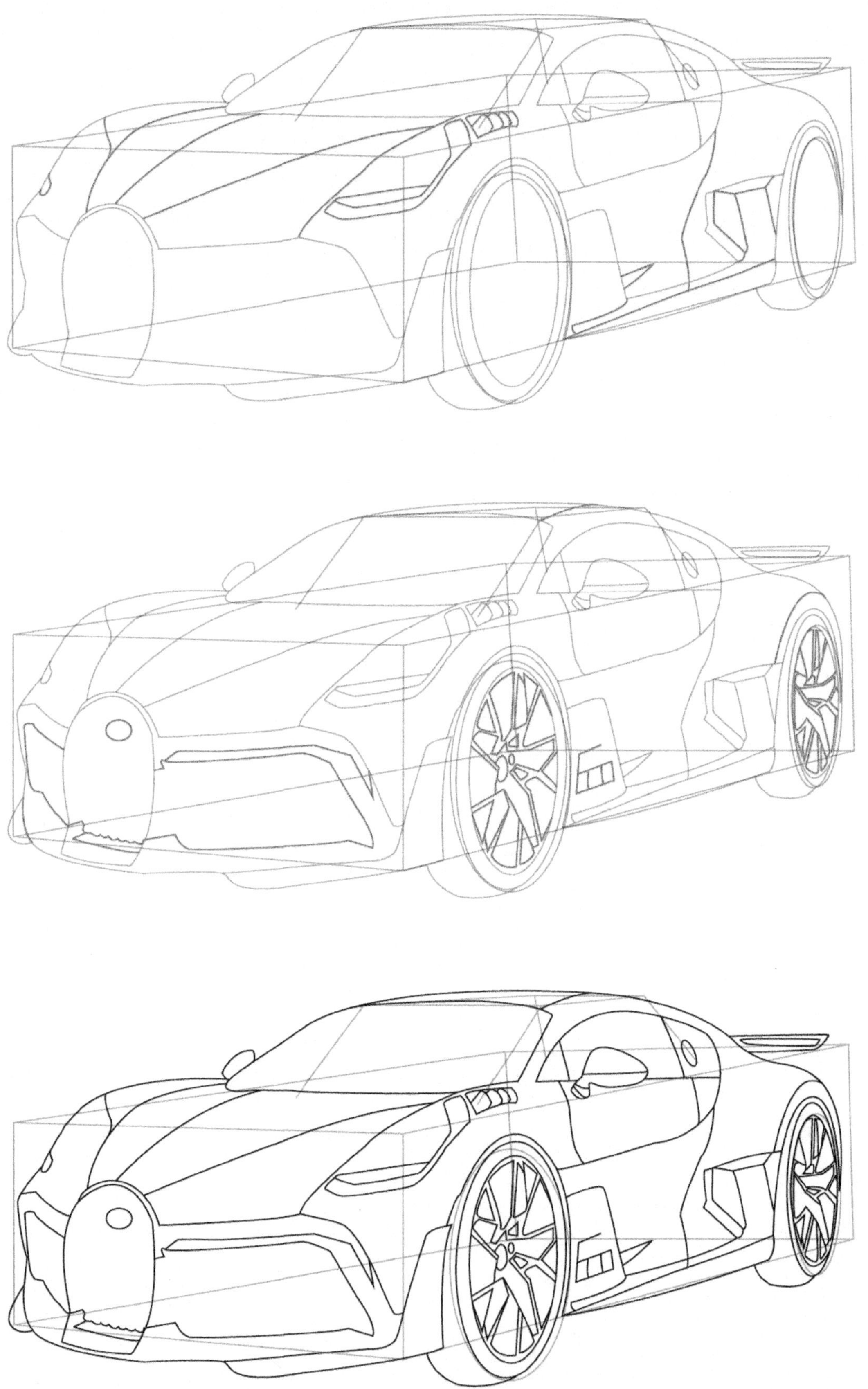

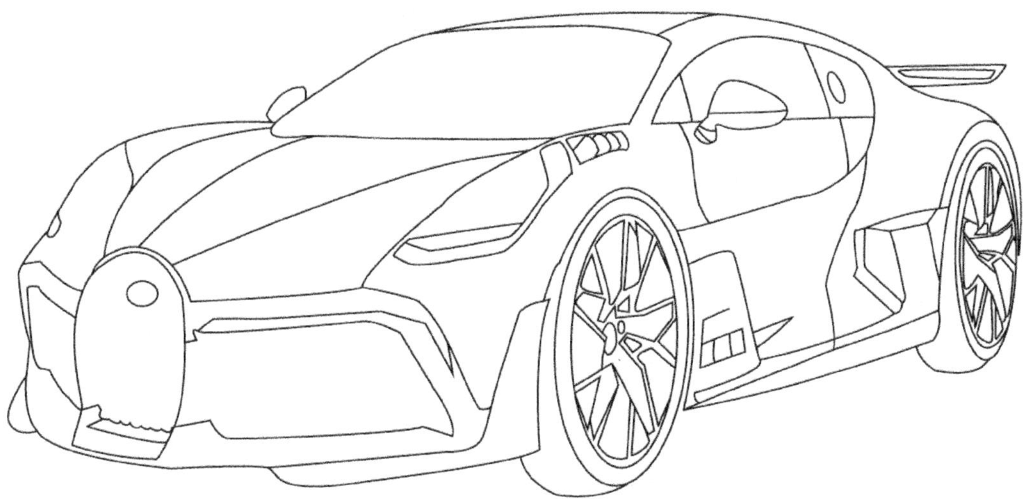

Chevelle SS

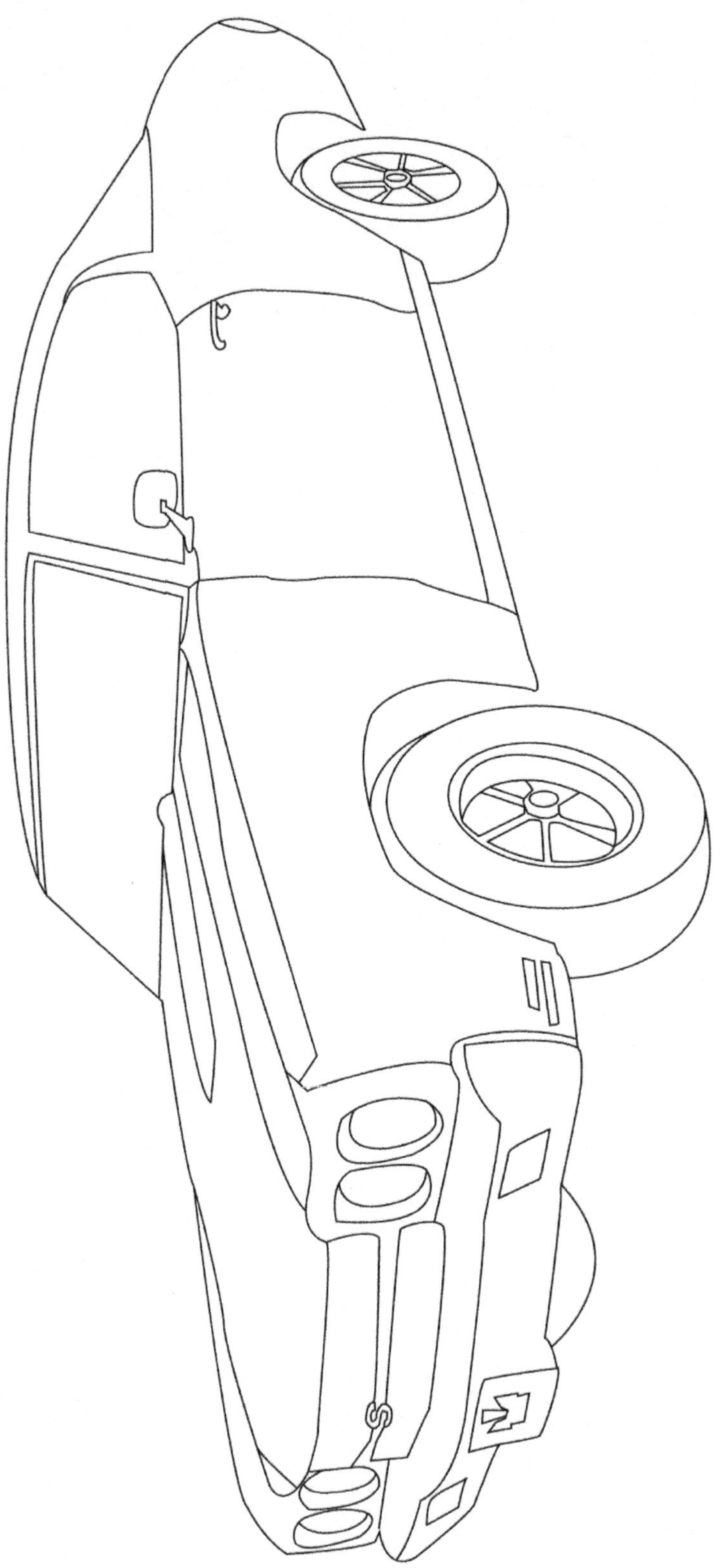

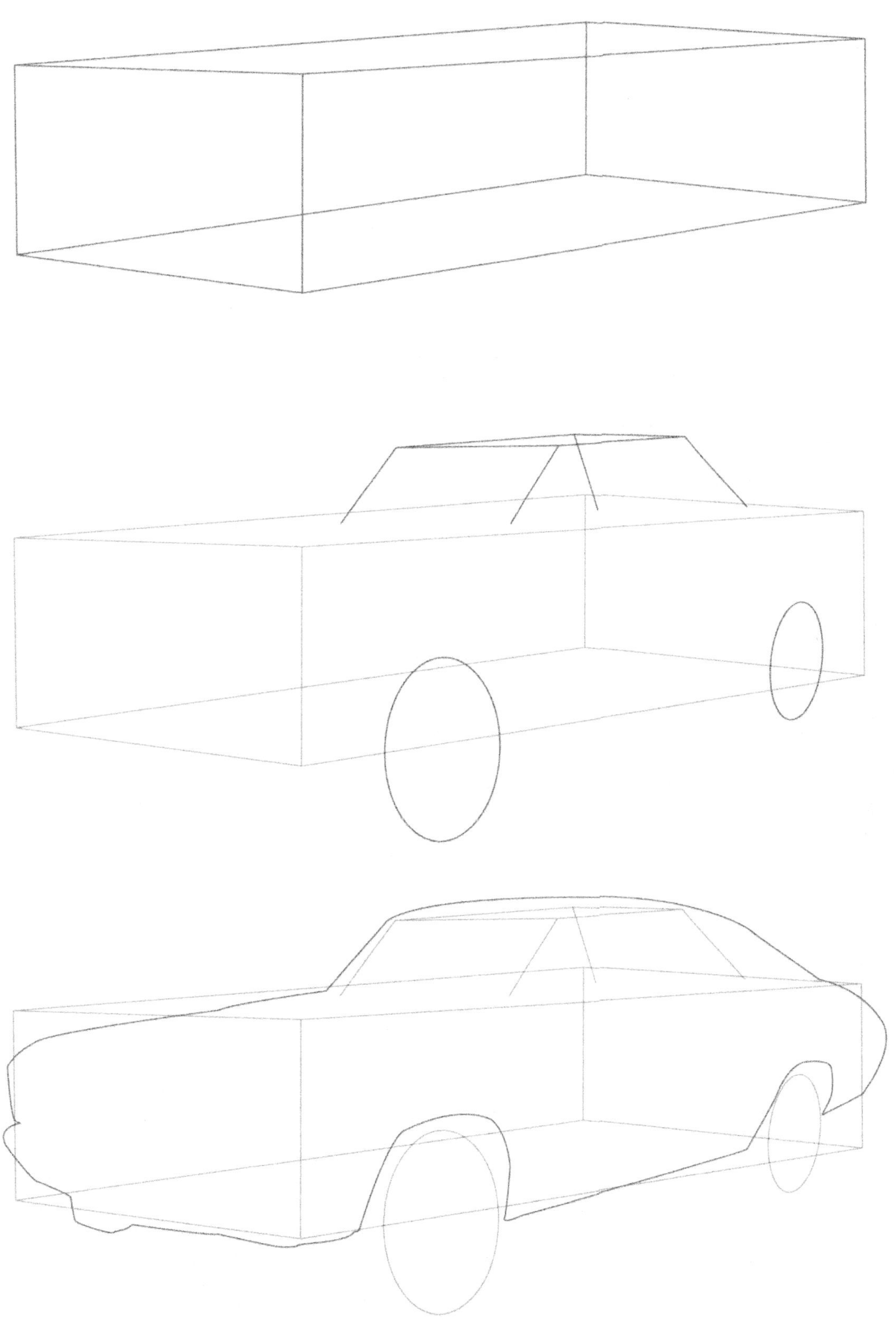

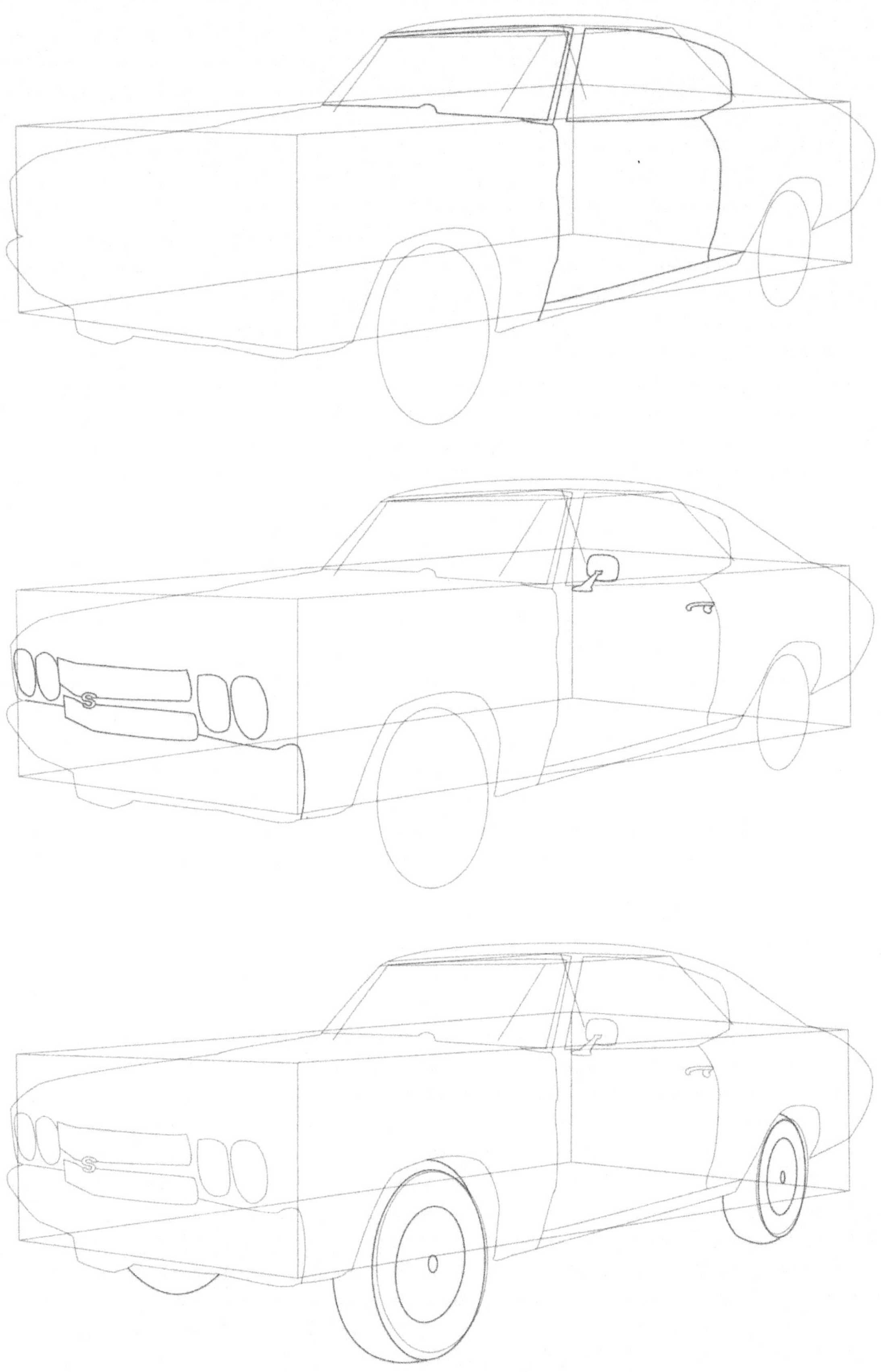

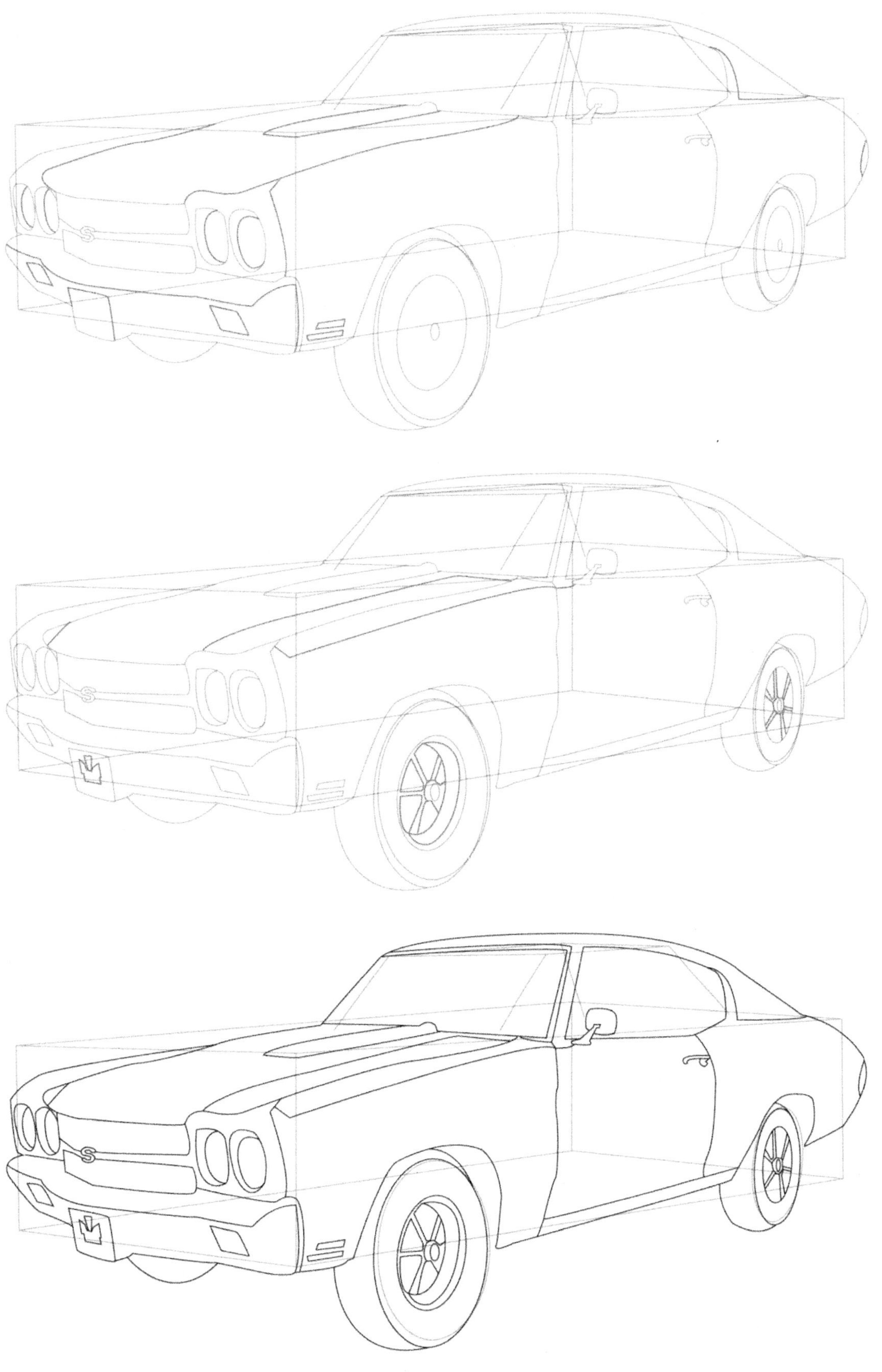

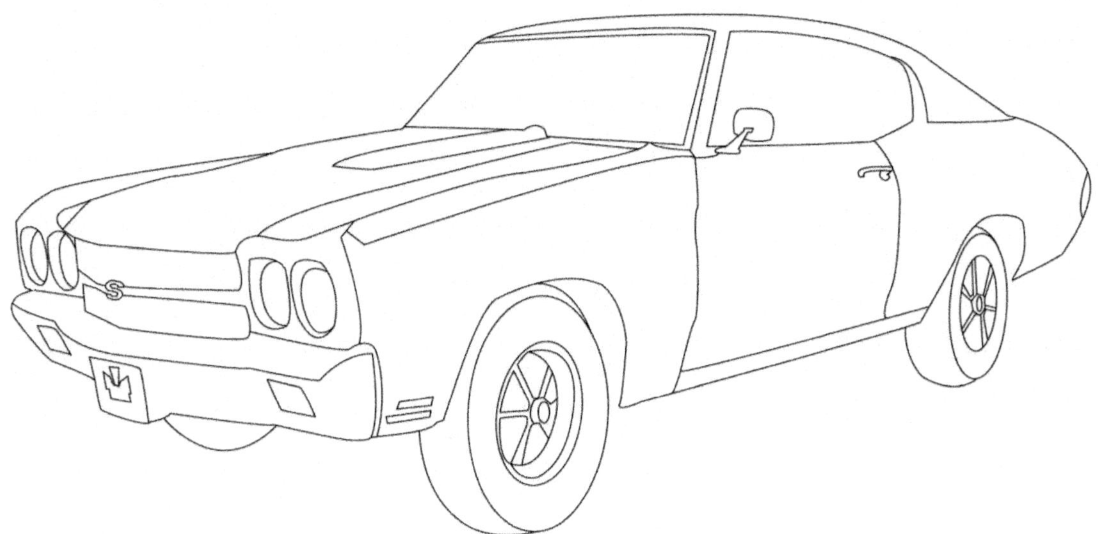

Dodge Viper SRT

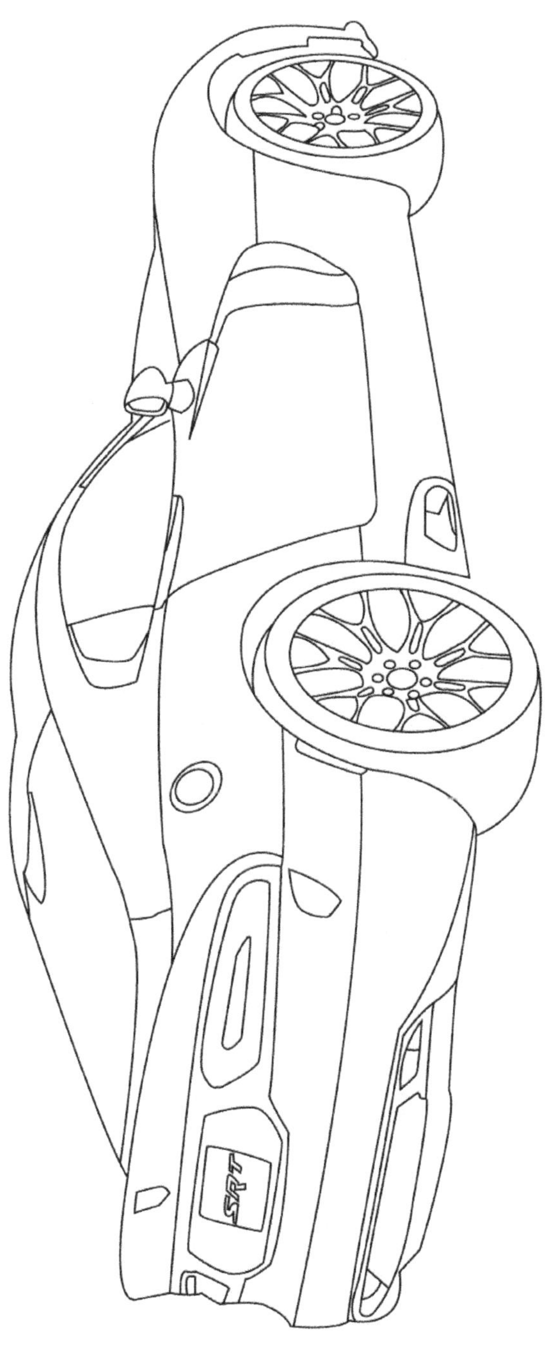

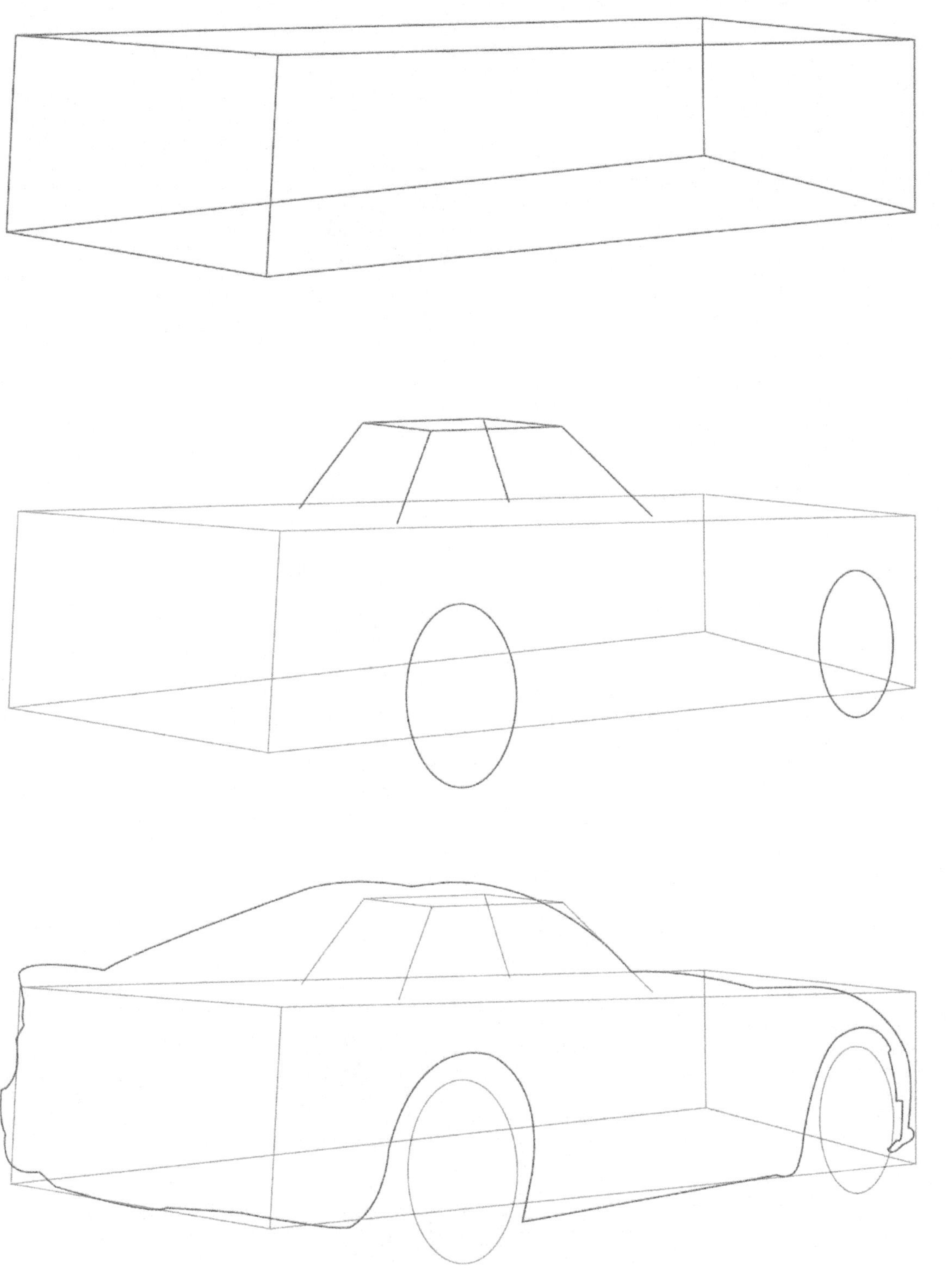

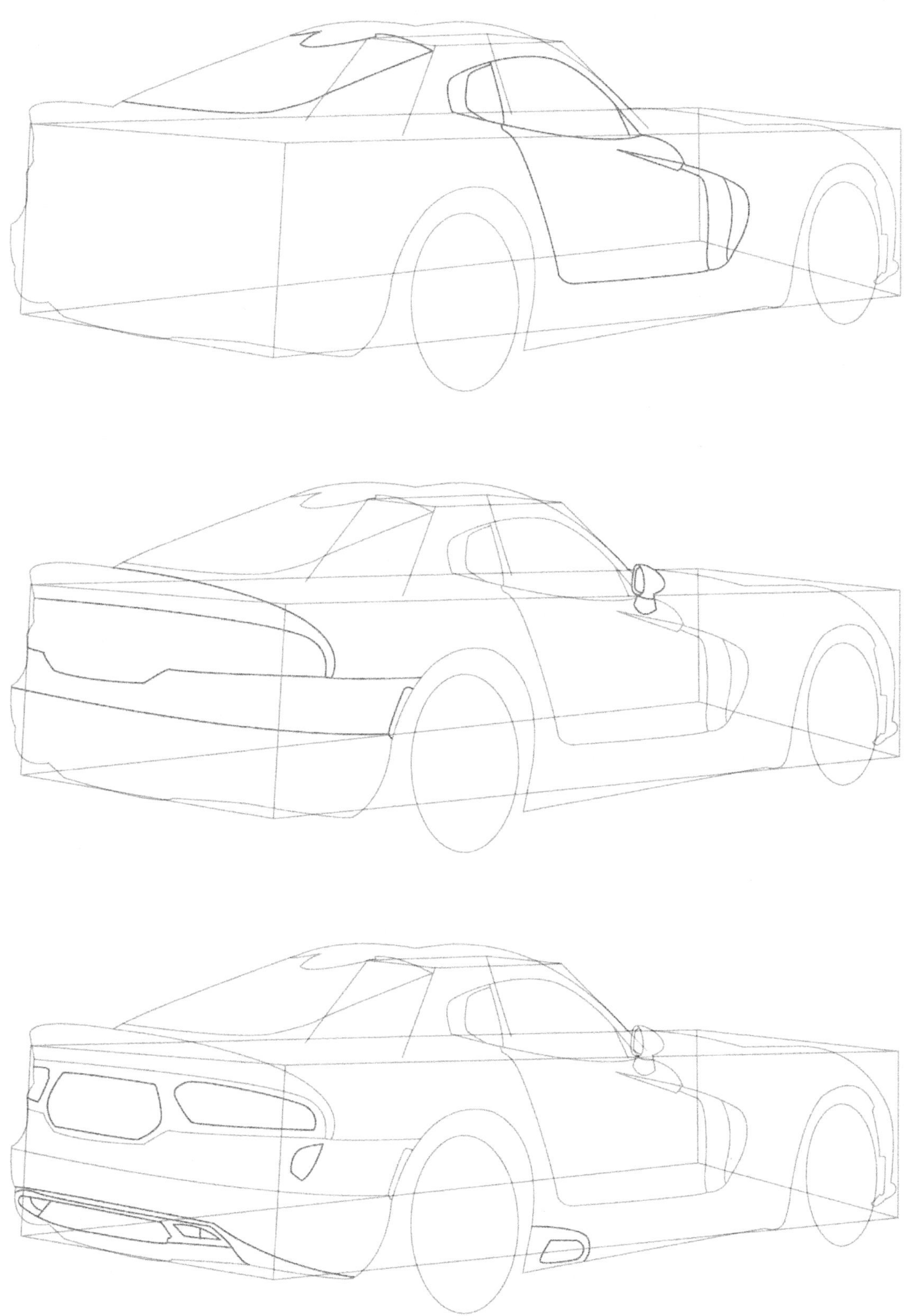

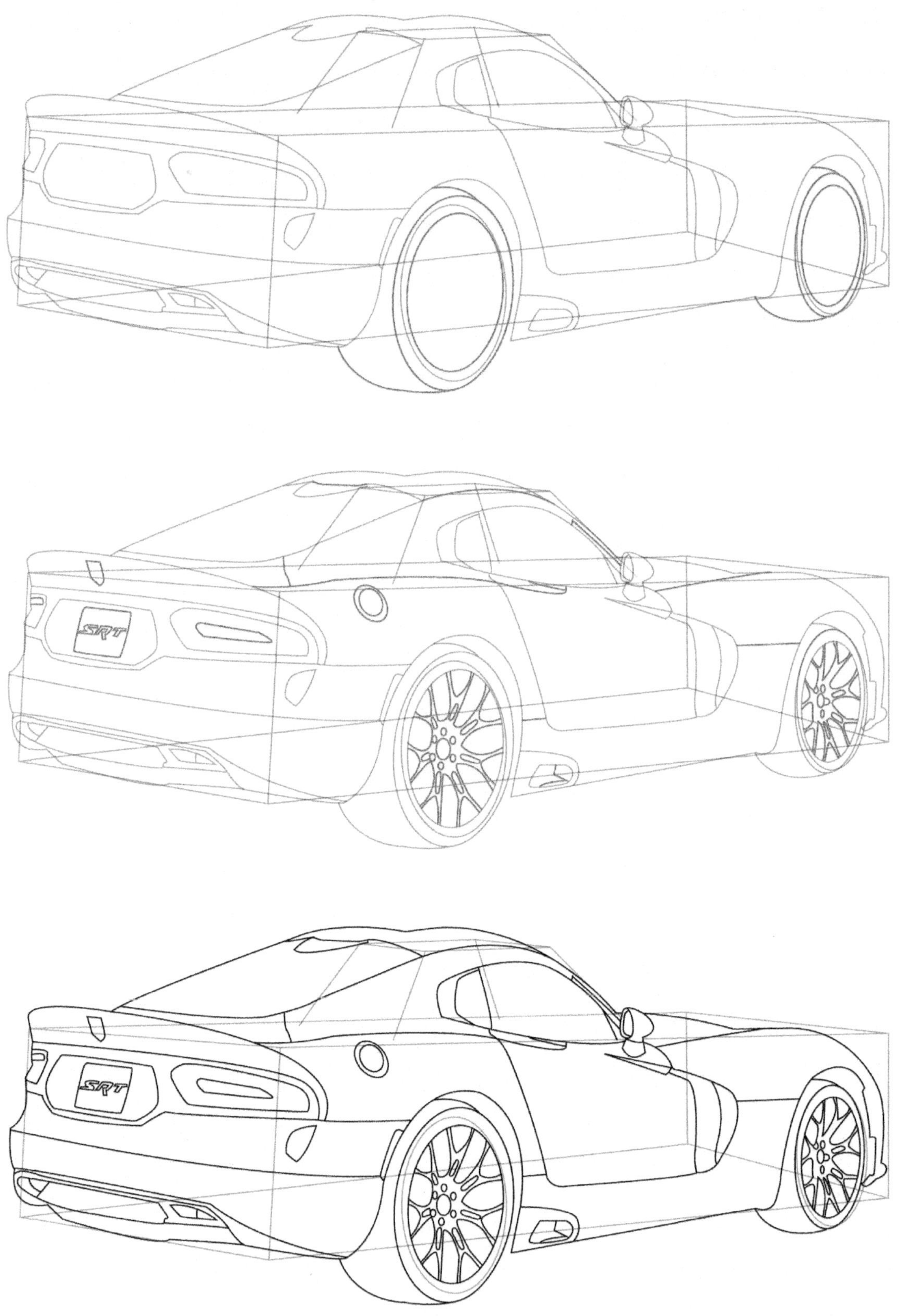
SRT
SRT

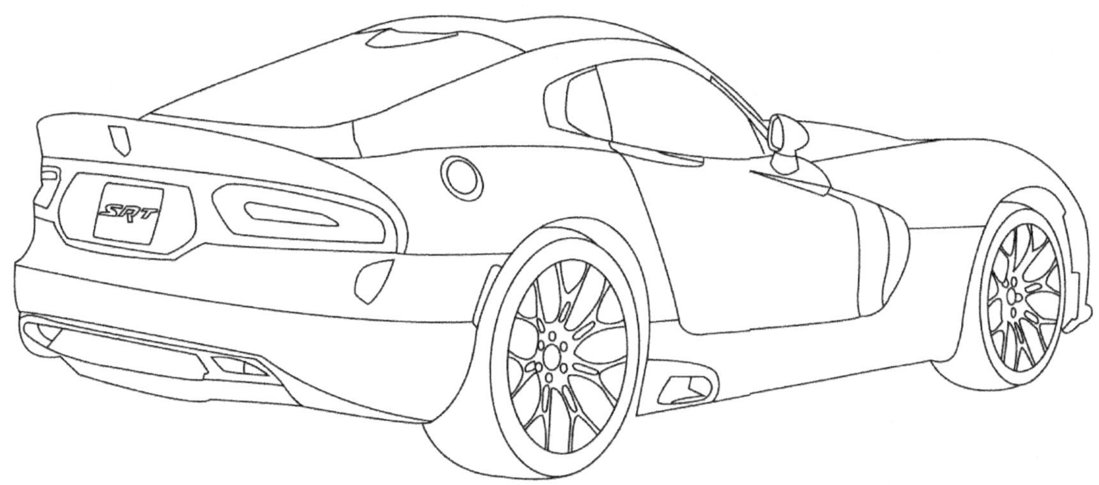
SRT

Ford GT

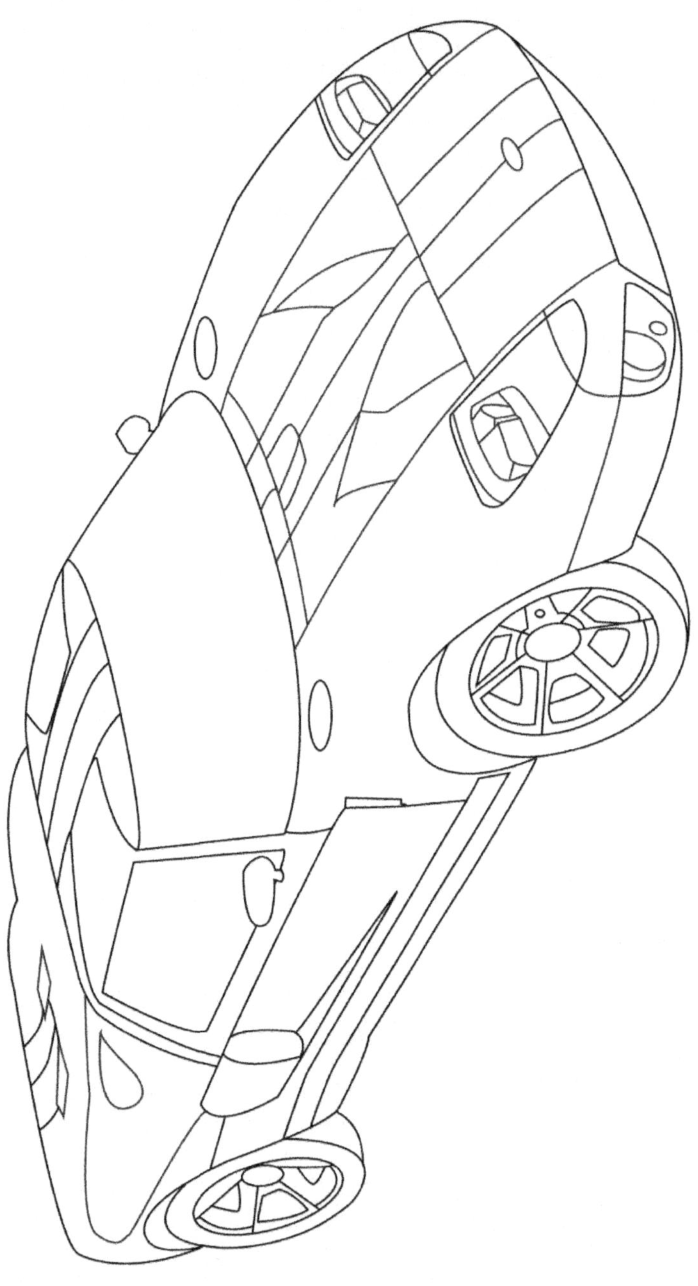

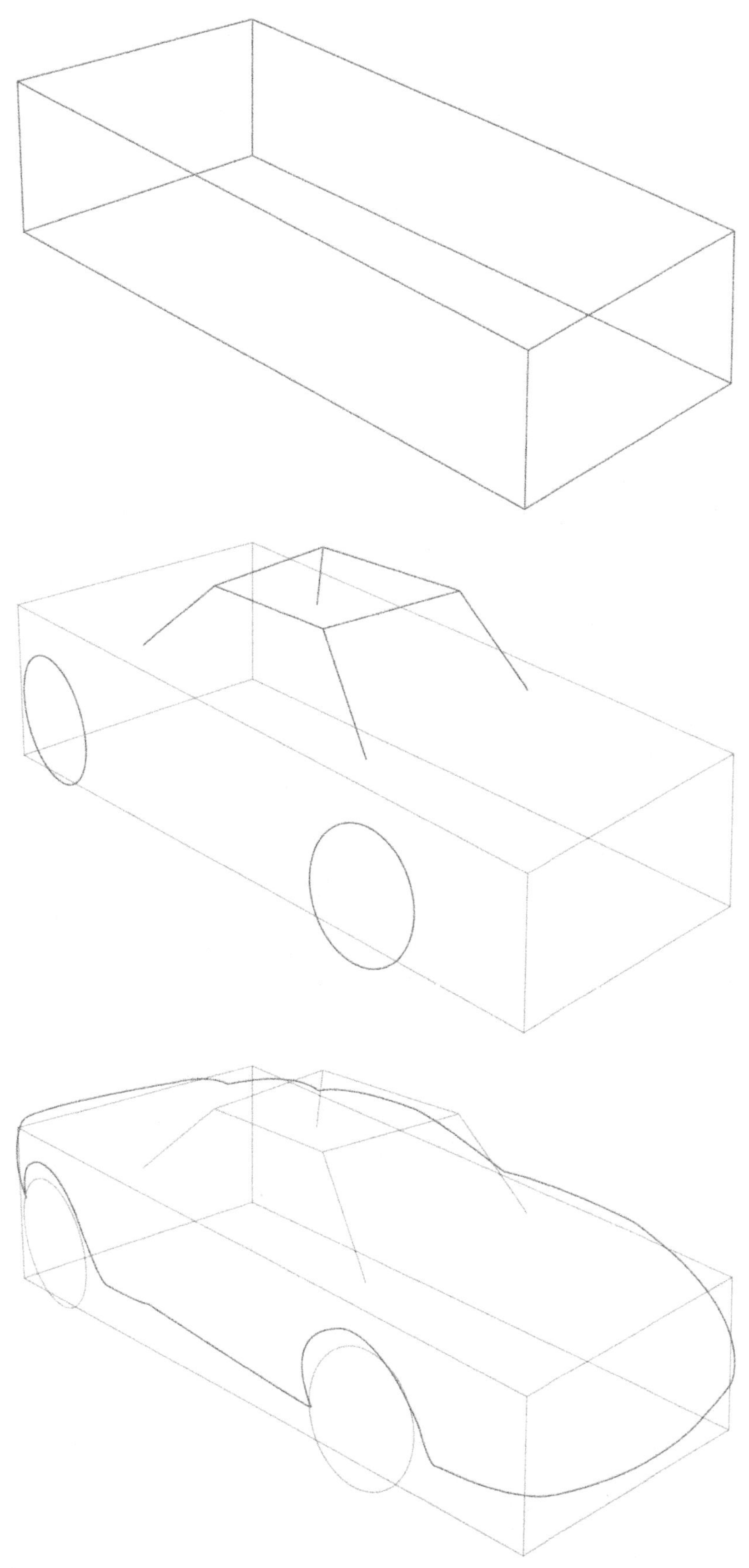

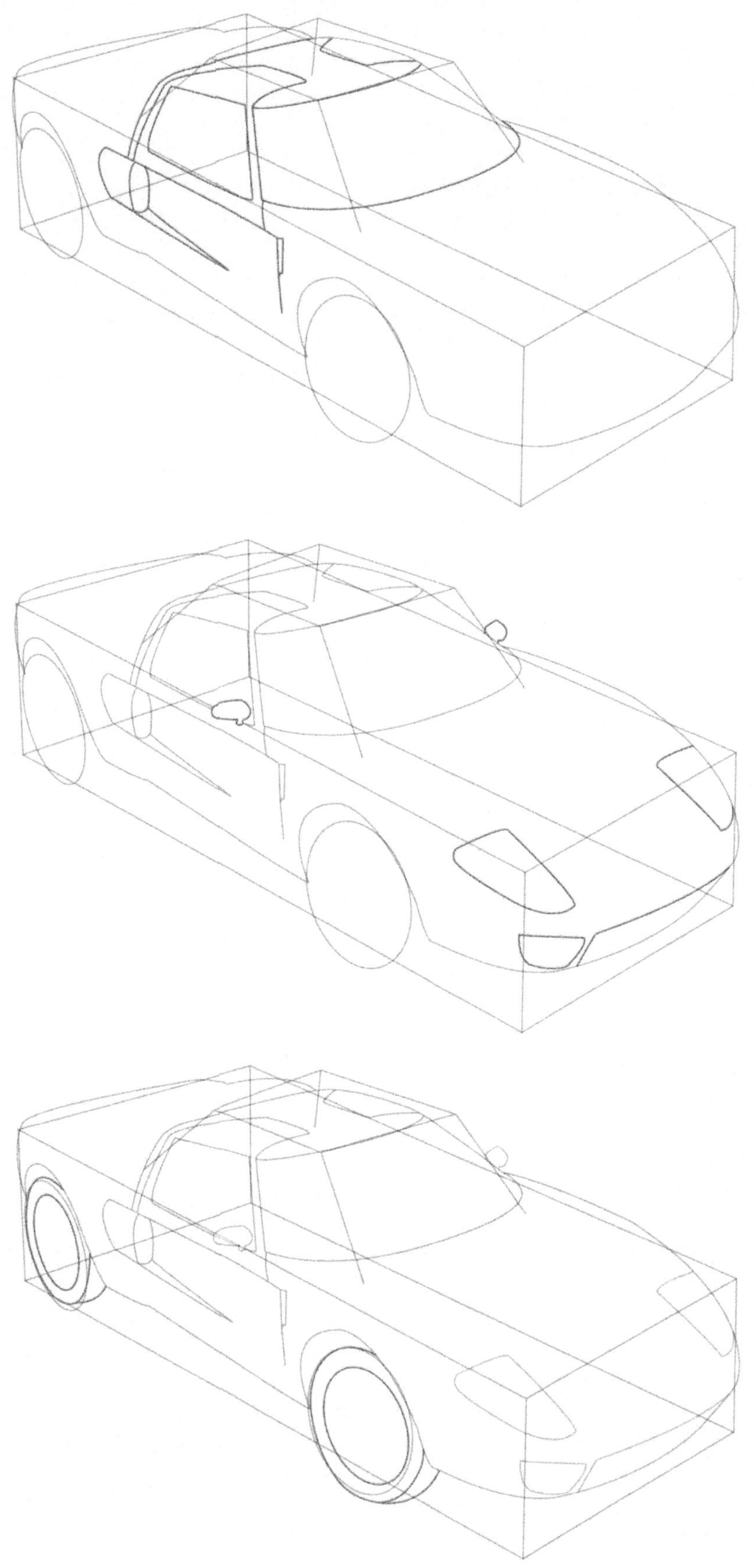

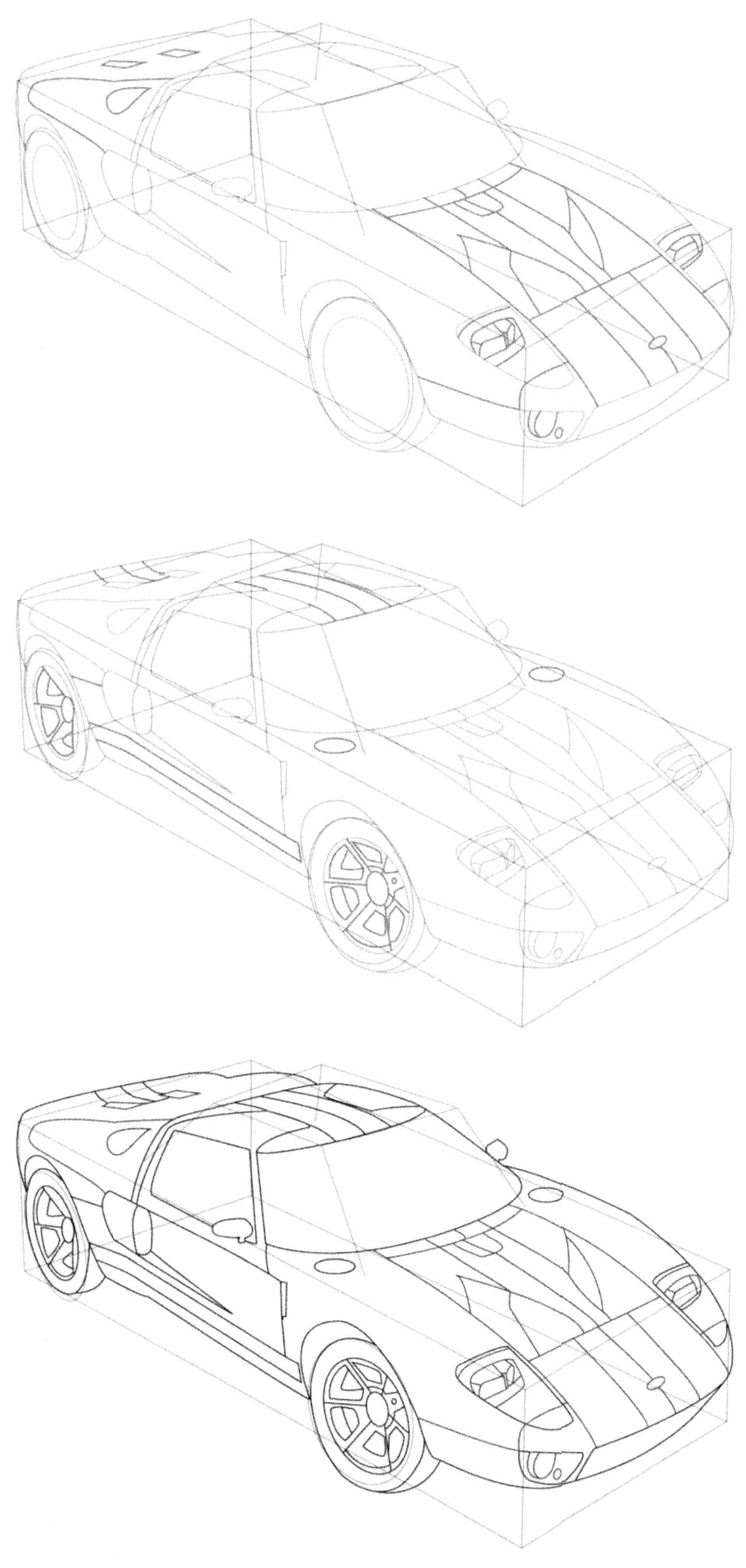

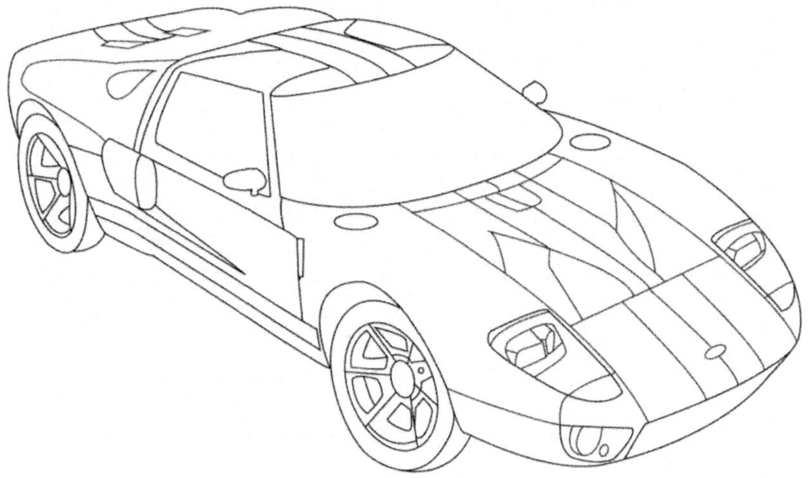

Bugatti Chiron

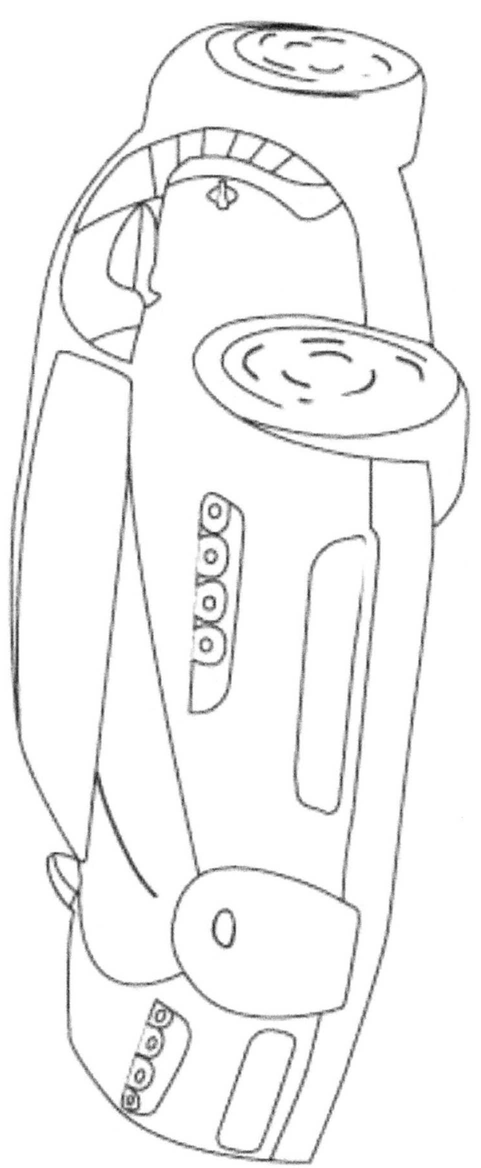

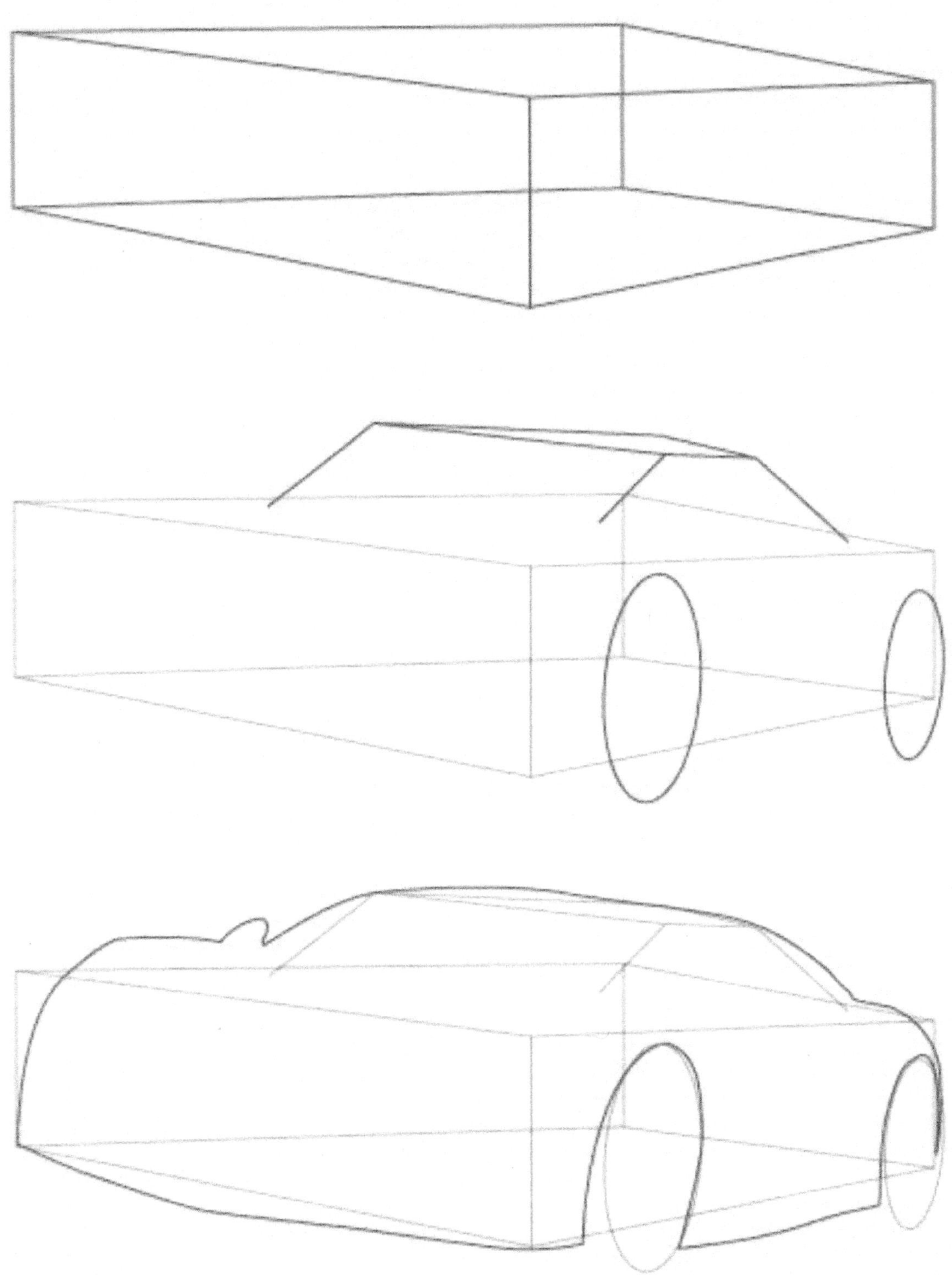

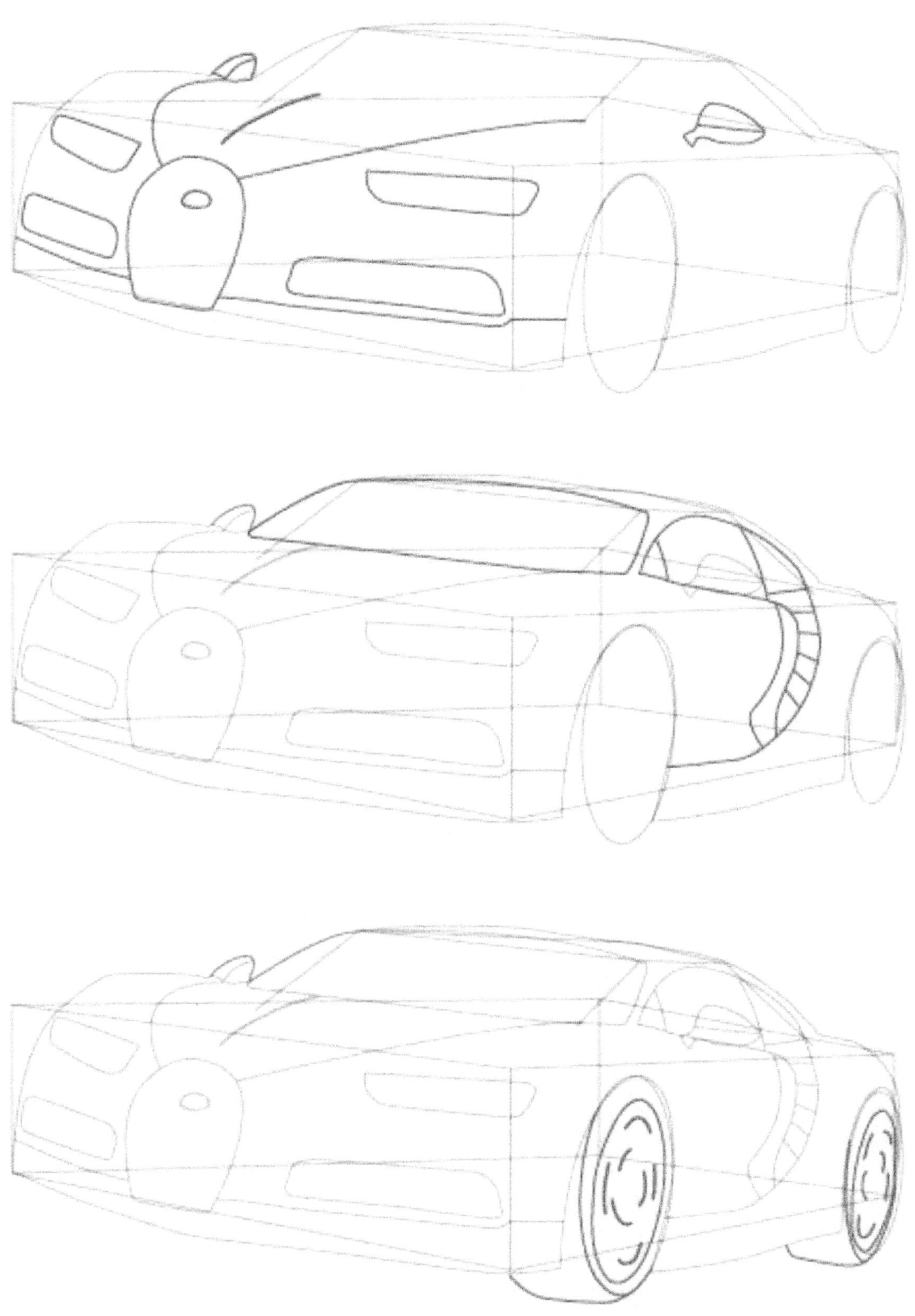

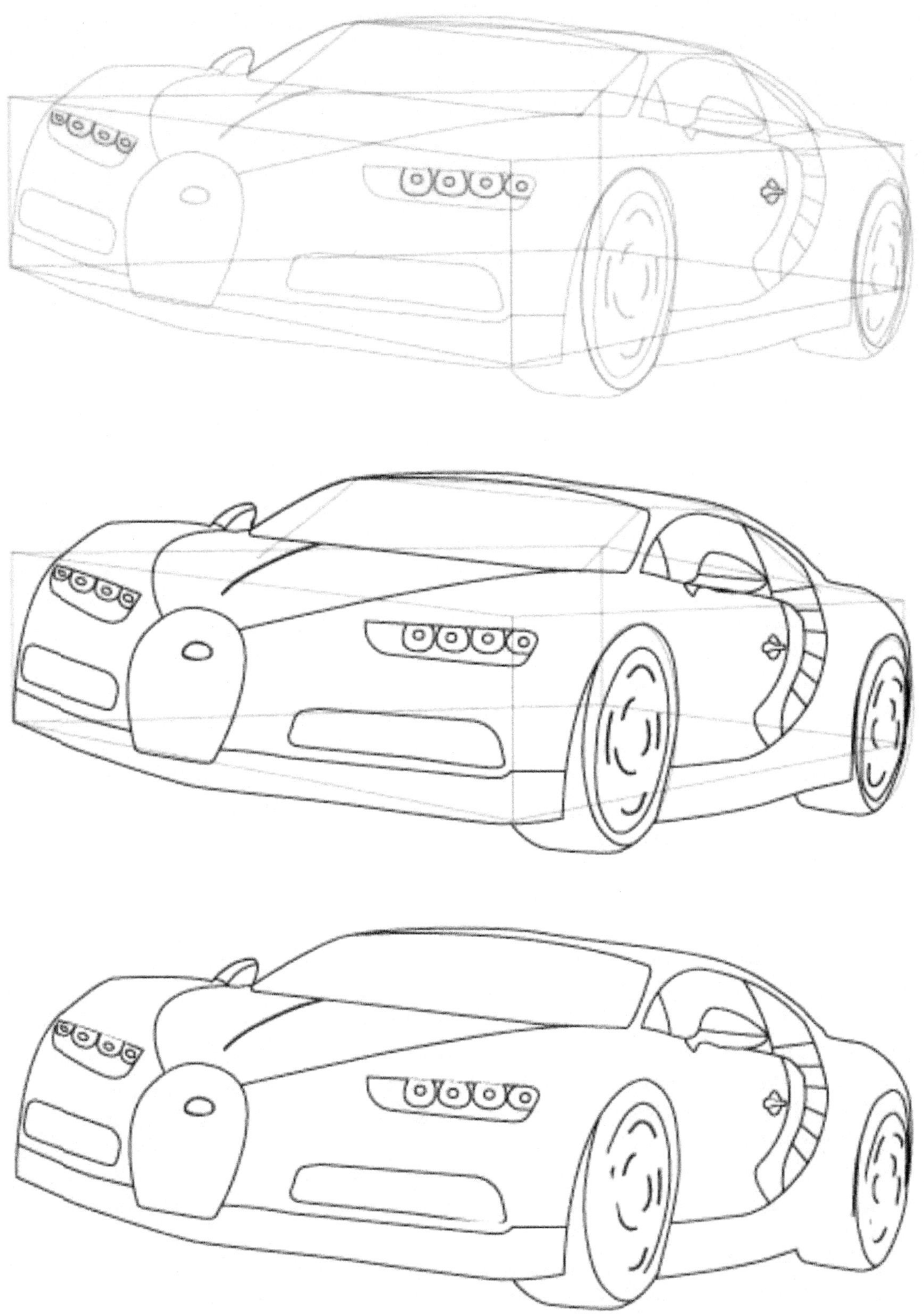

Audi R8 V10

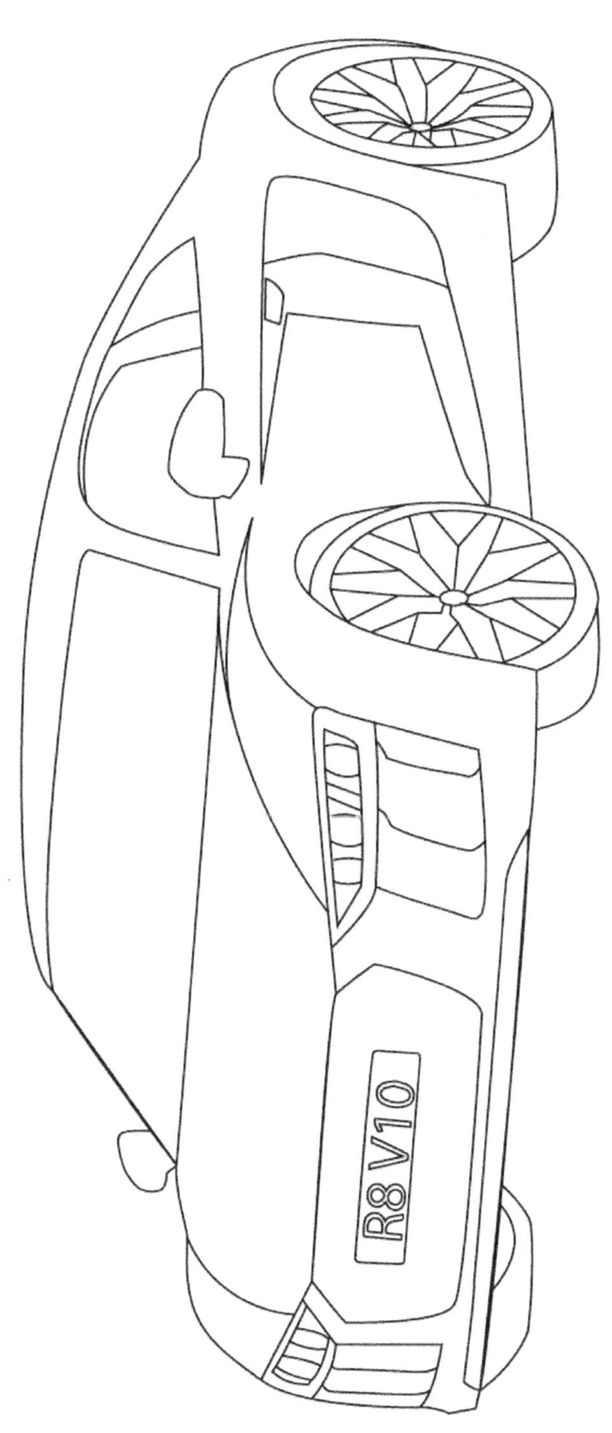

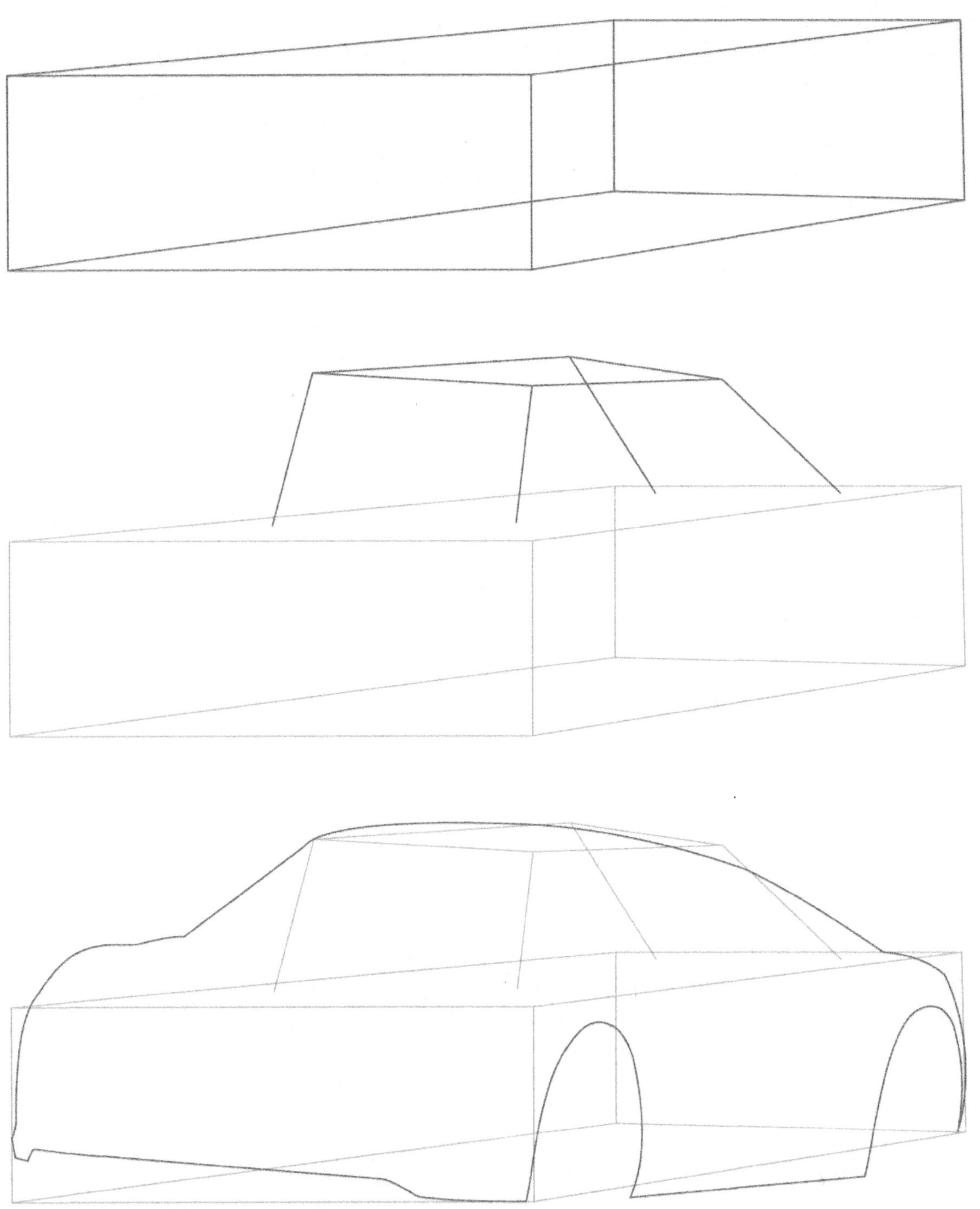

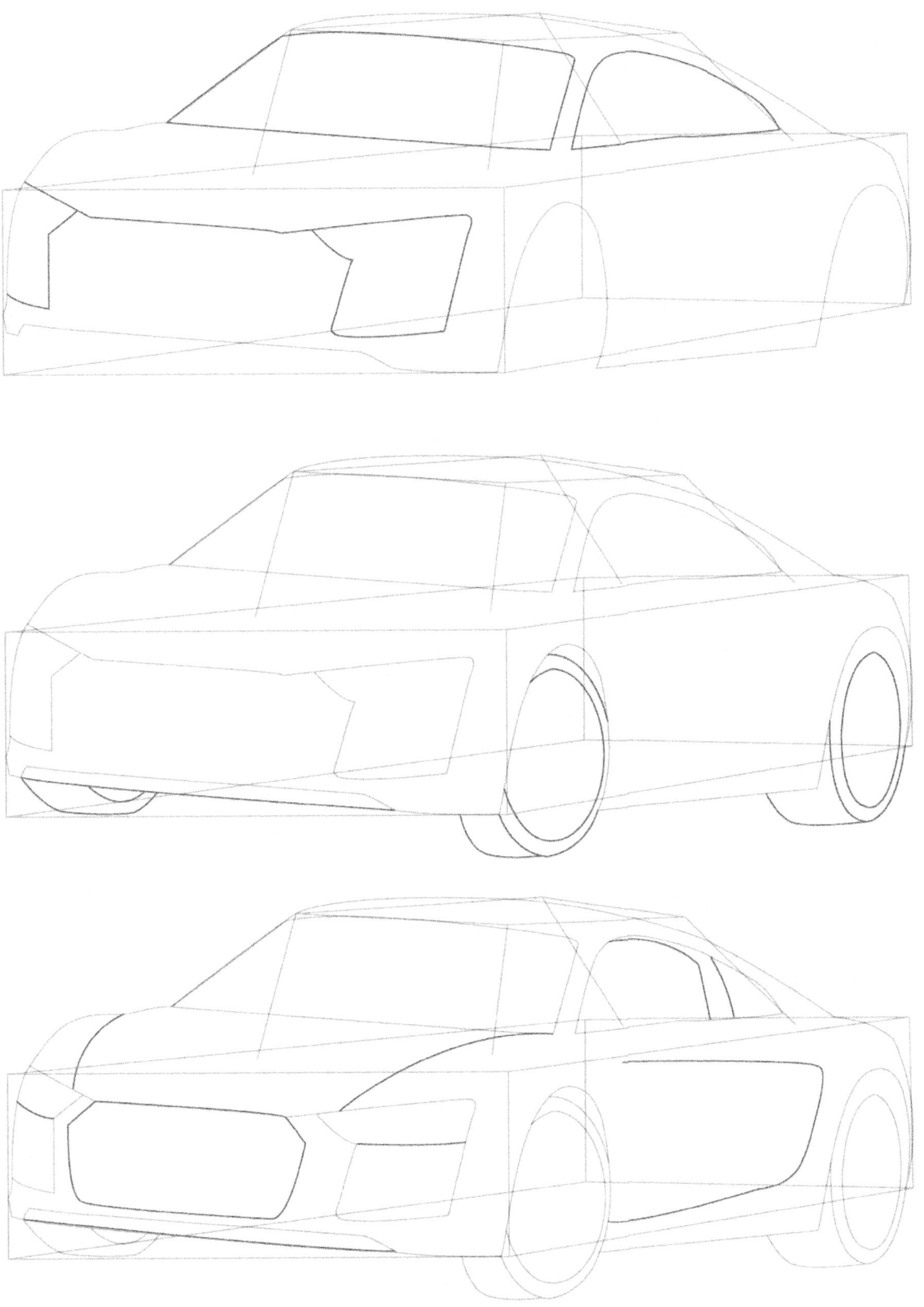

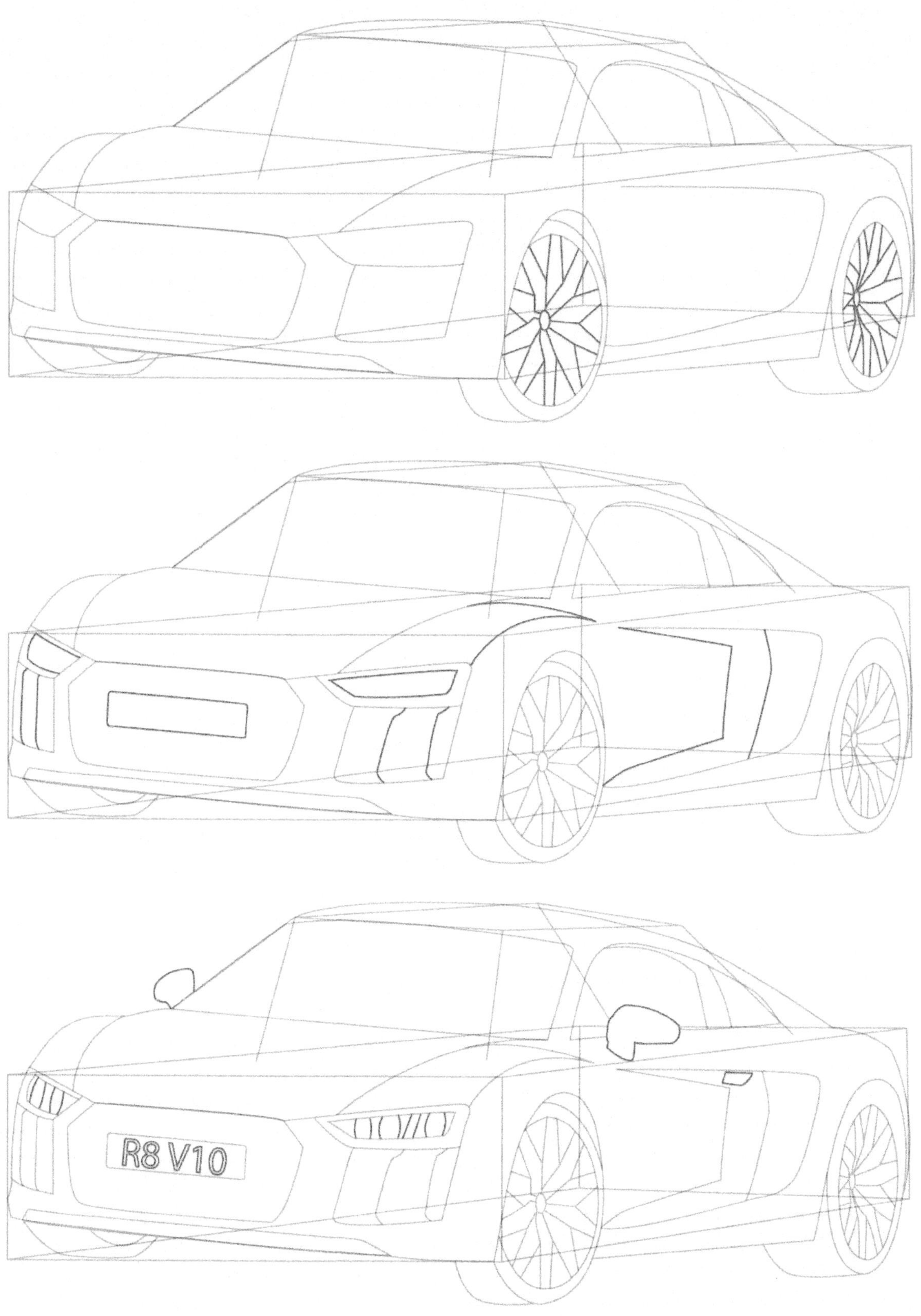
R8 V10

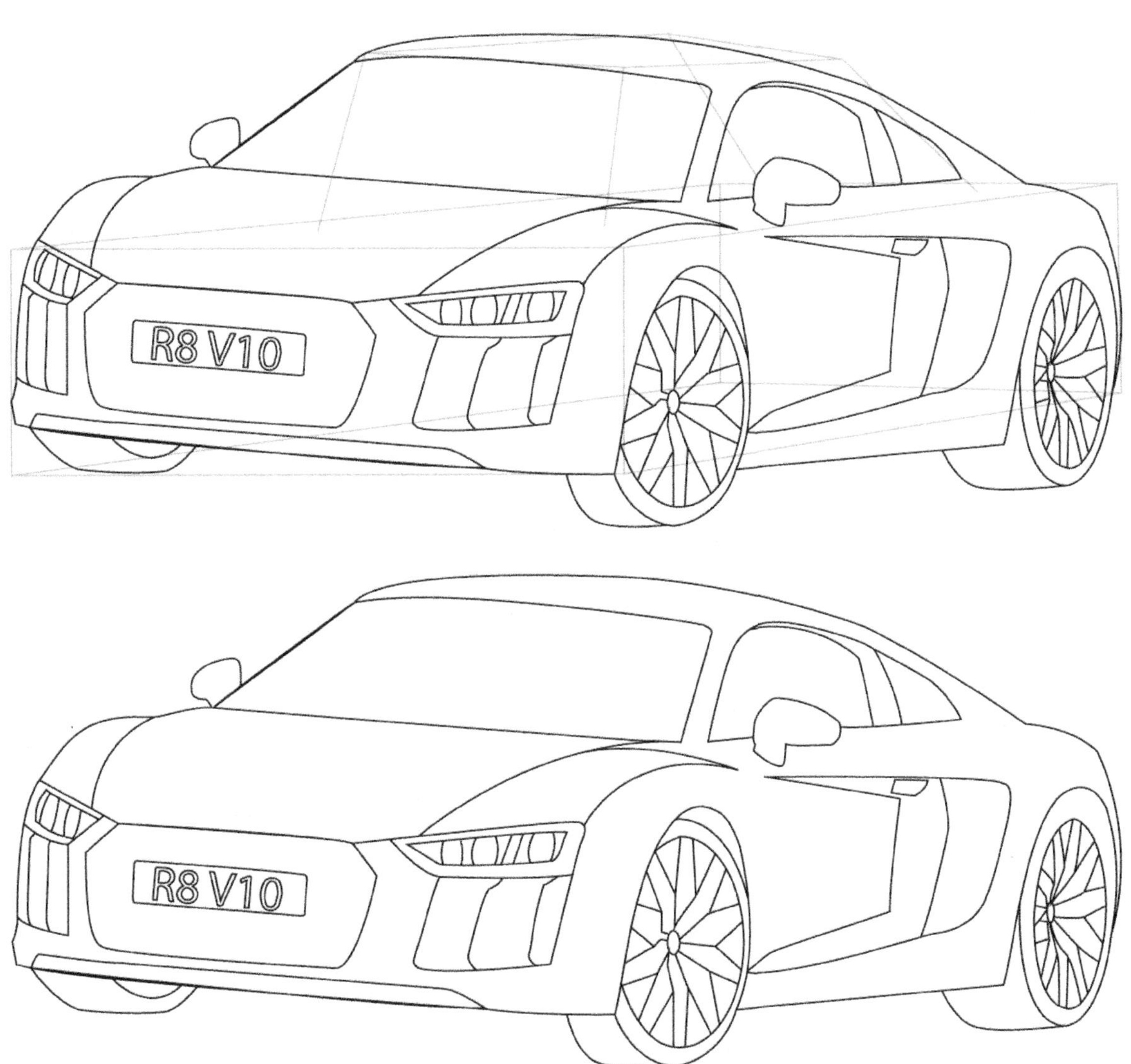
R8 V10
R8 V10

McLaren 570S

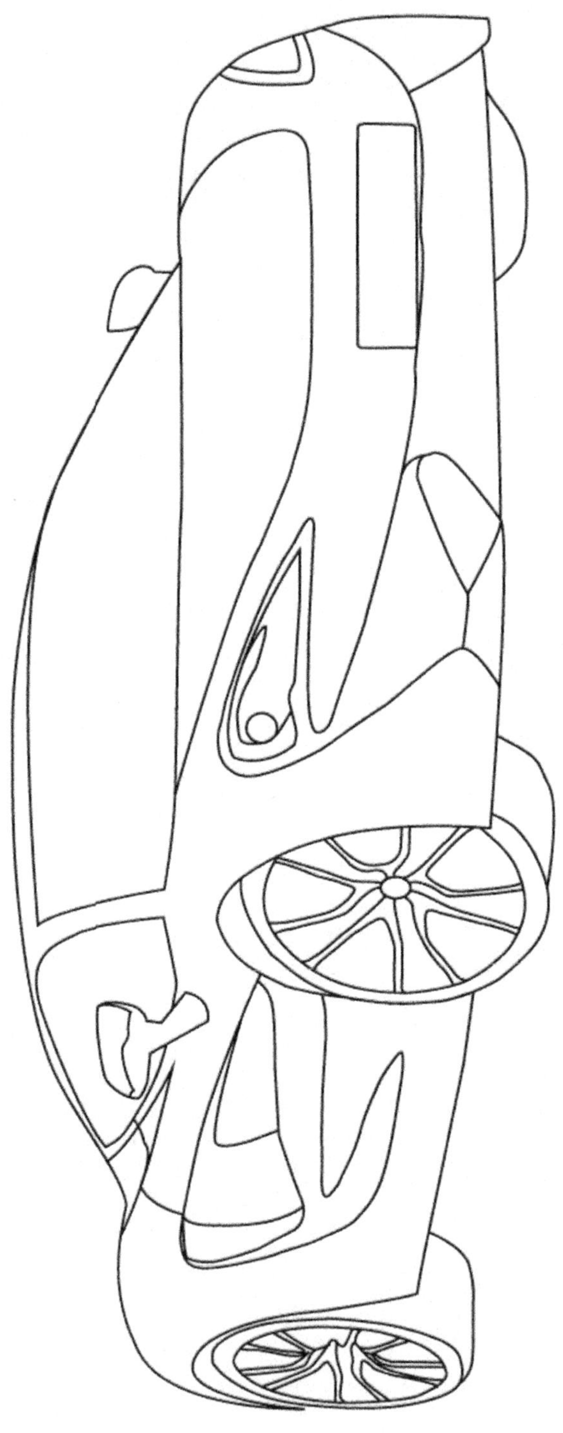

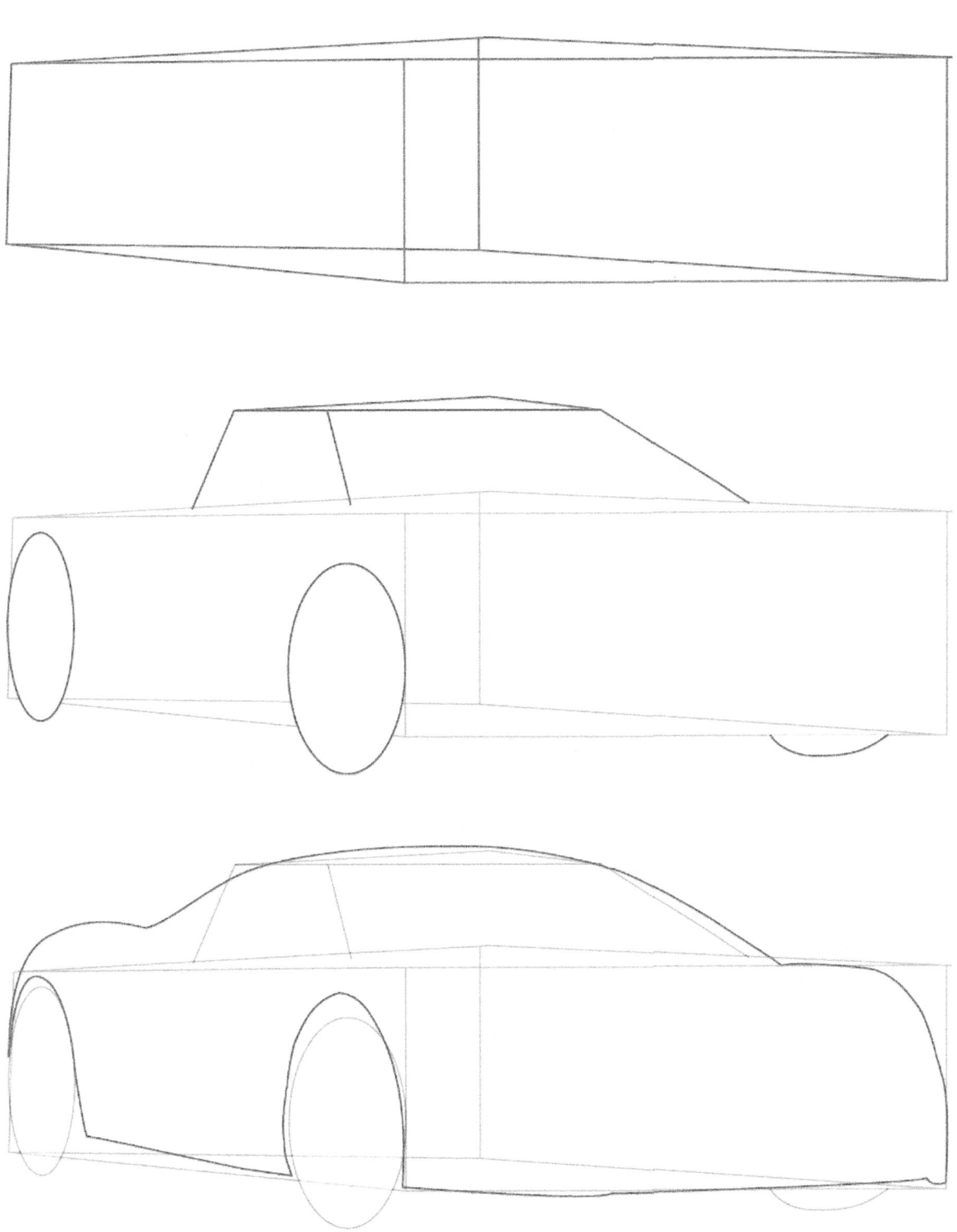

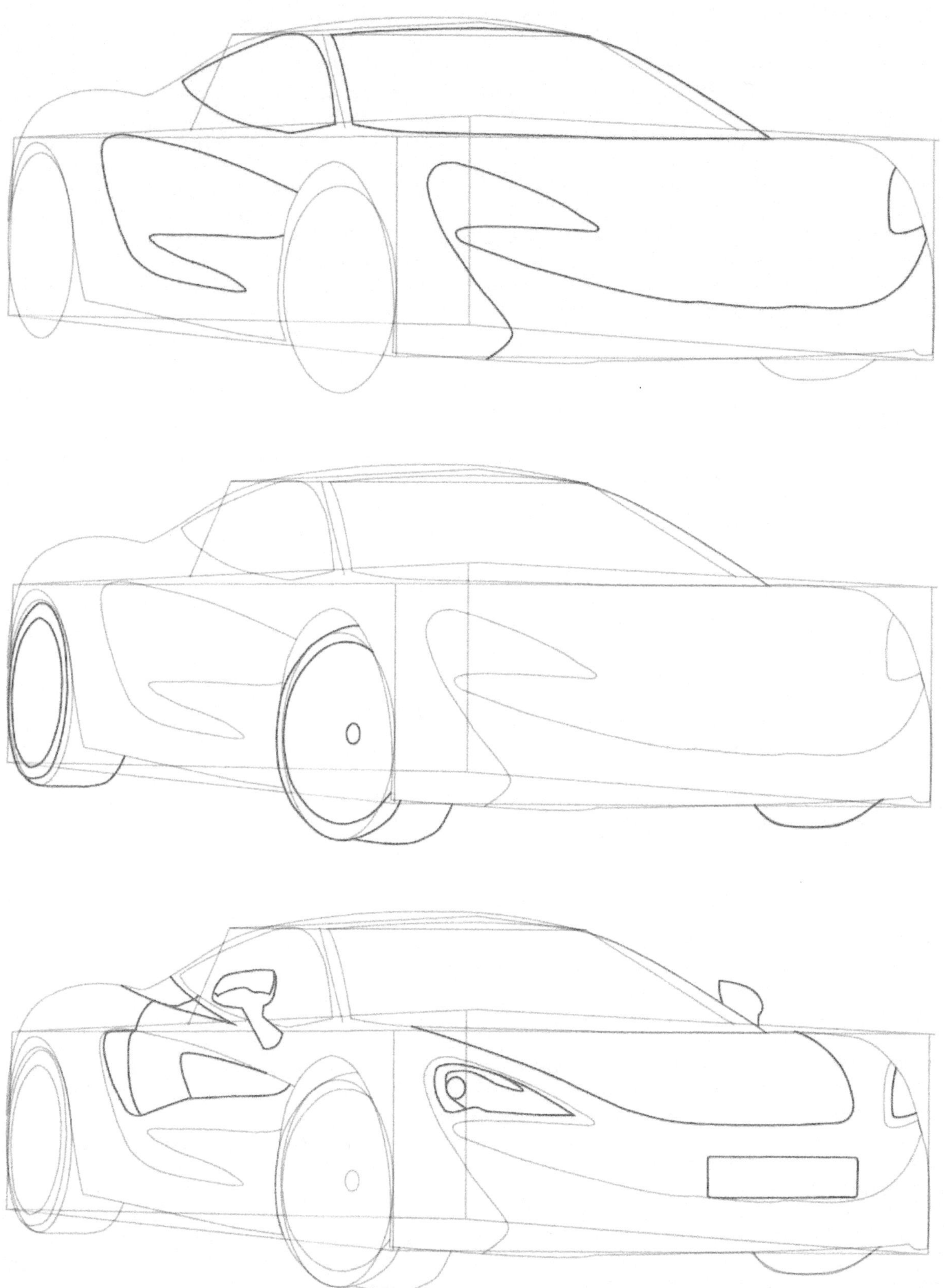

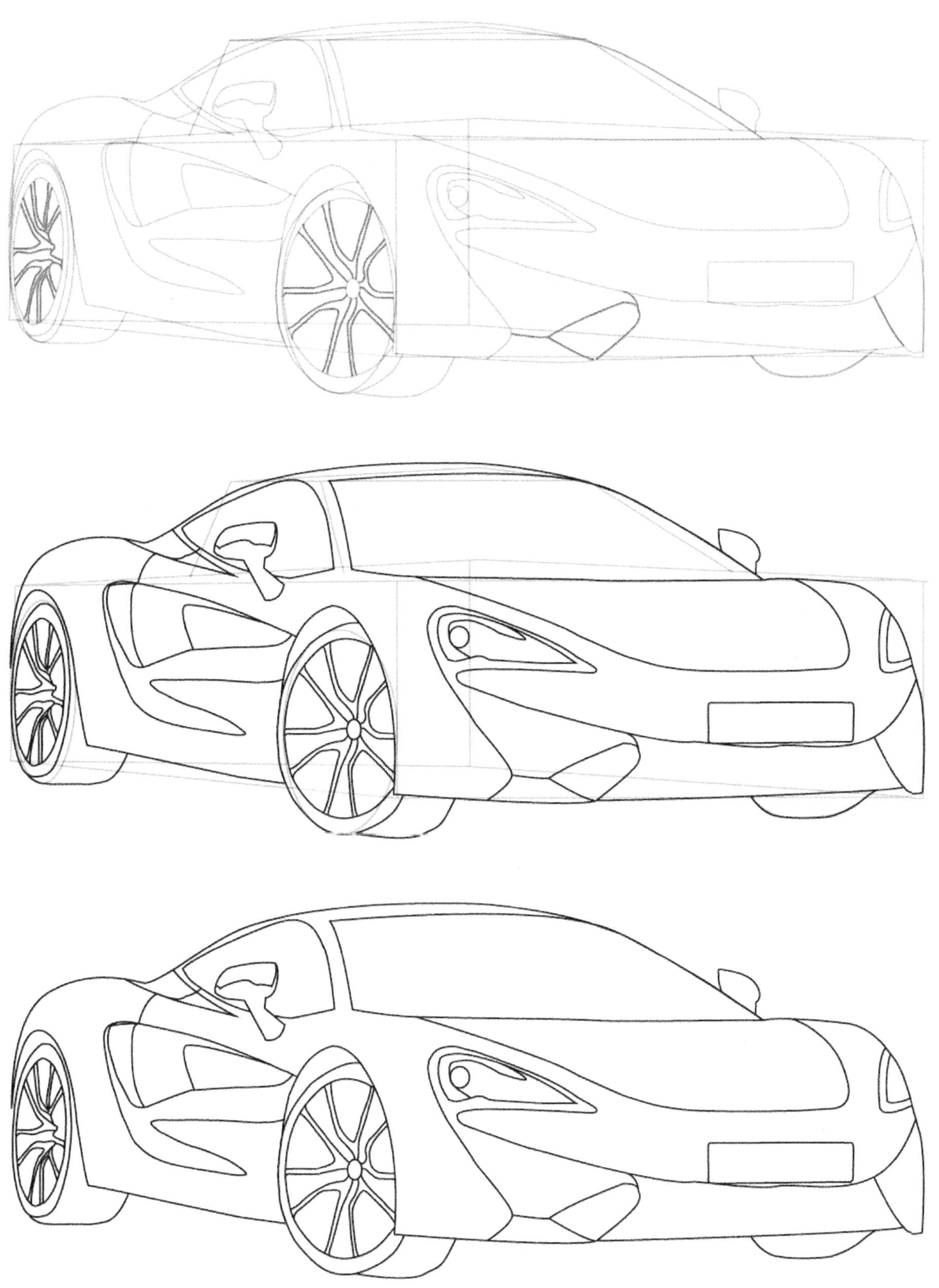

HEY... THANK YOU FOR BEING AWESOME.

WE HOPE THAT YOU HAVE FUN TIME WITH YOUR BOOK. WE HAVE GIFT FOR YOU. YOU CAN DOWNLOAD A FREE PRINTABLE SET OF OUR BEST COLORING PAGES BY VISITING OUR WEBSITE :

AMBERFORREST.COM

IT WOULD BE SO COOL IF YOU COULD SHARE YOUR COMPLETED IMAGES WITH US. YOU CAN TAG US ON

FACEBOOK & INSTAGRAM
@COLORWITHAMBER

WE ARE ALWAYS WORKING HARD TO IMPROVE OUR BOOKS. PLEASE LET US KNOW HOW WE ARE DOING BY WRITING A REVIEW OF OUR BOOK ON YOUR FAVORITE ONLINE STORE.

Made in the USA
Middletown, DE
29 May 2021

40671558R00060

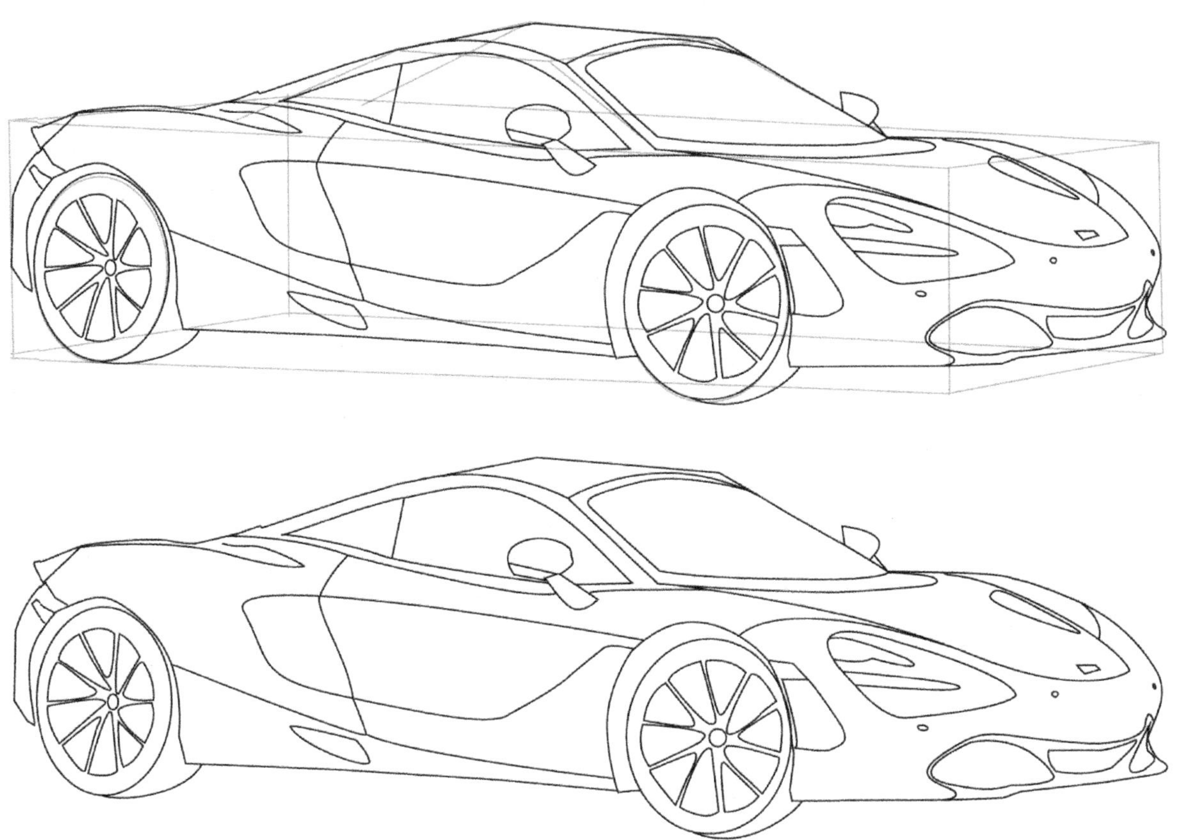

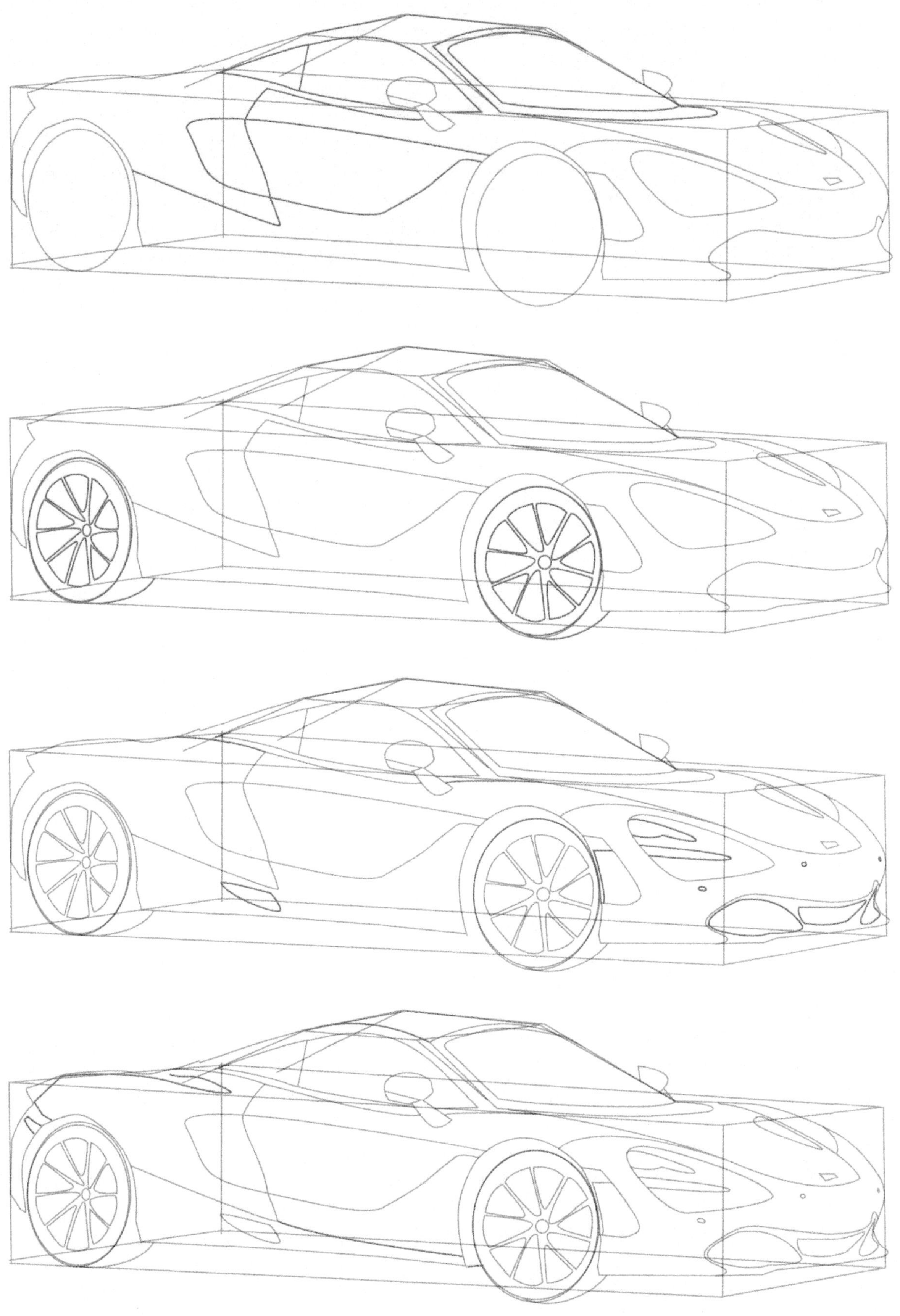

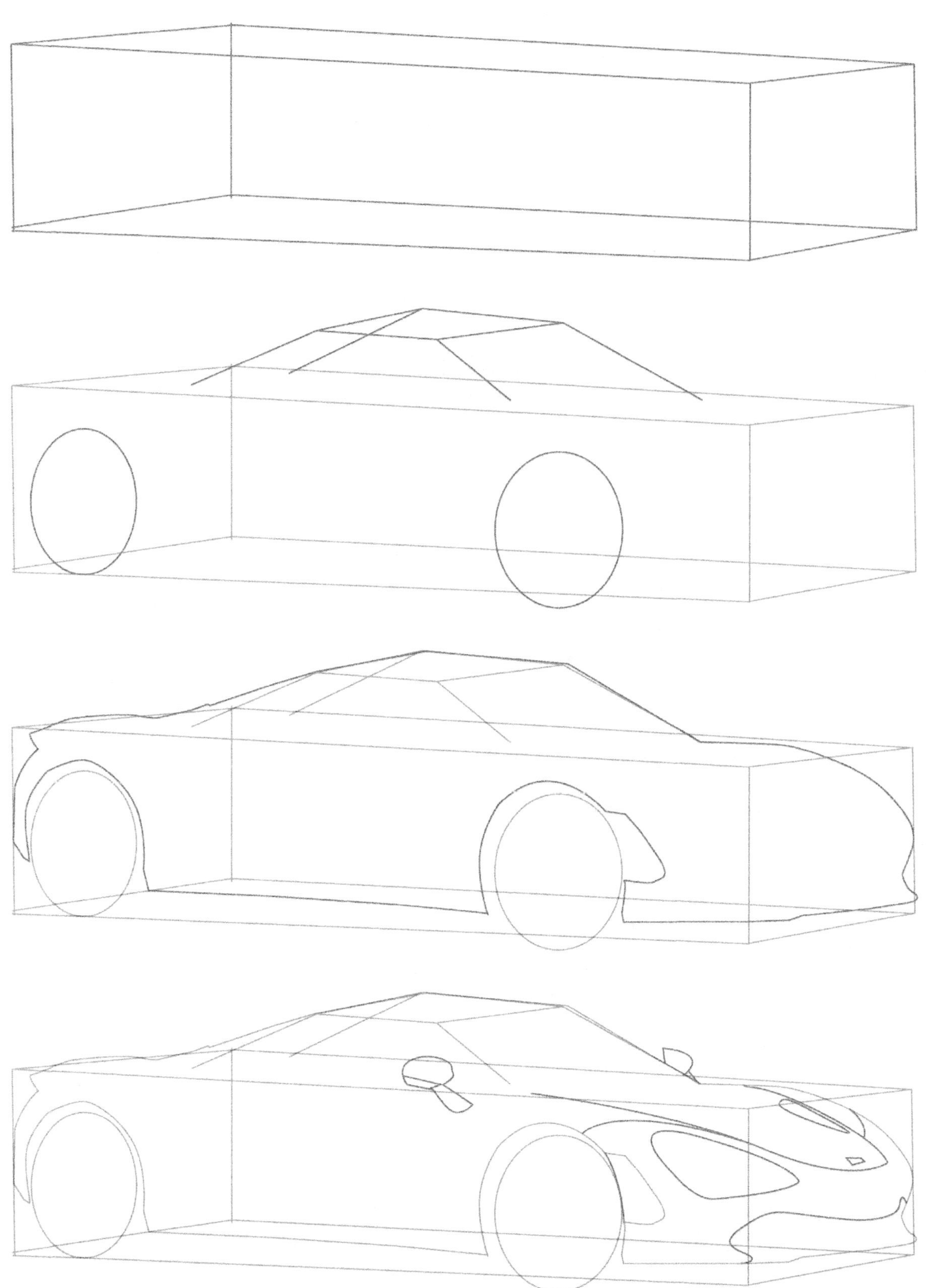

McLaren 720S

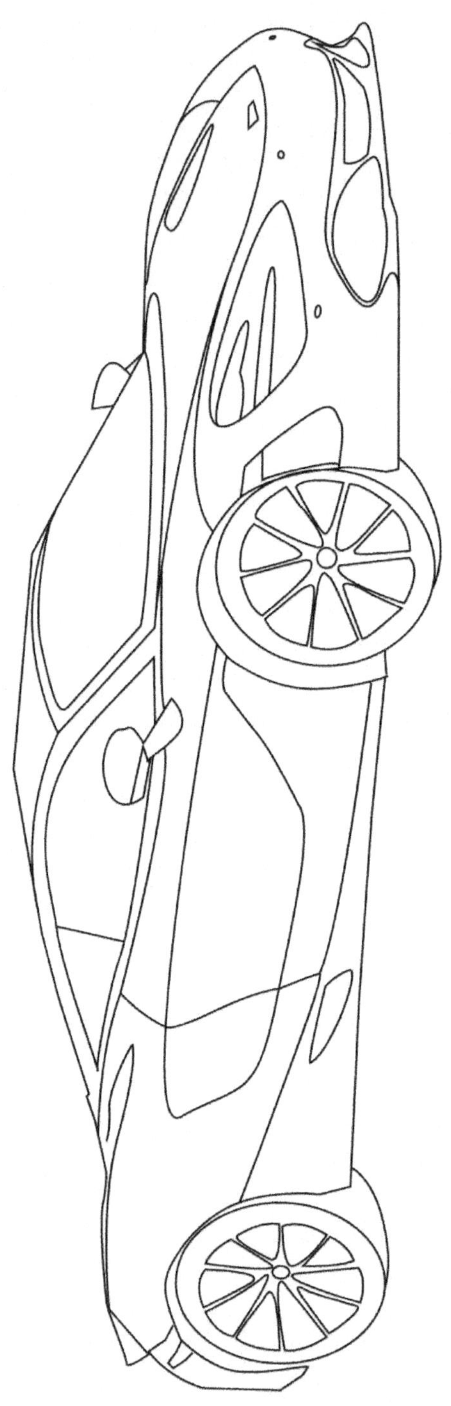

Contents

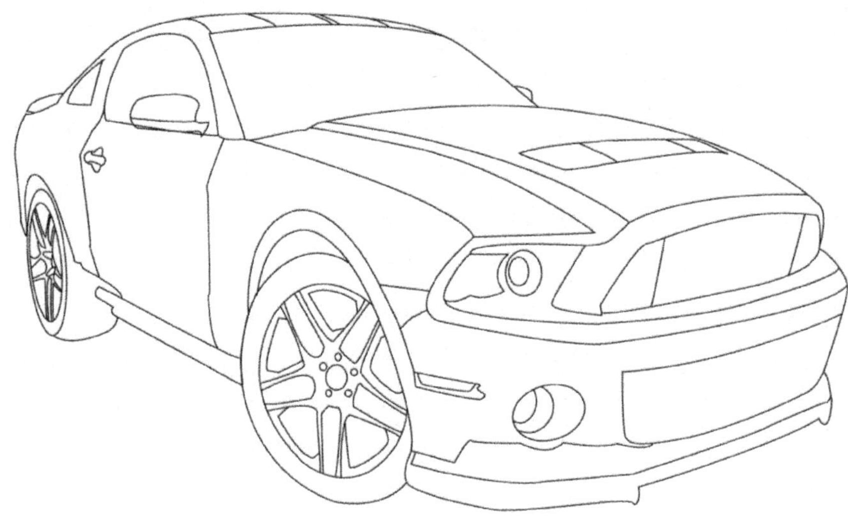

Drawing is a learned skill, one built over years of consistent practice. If you have the passion and commitment, you can take your knack for scribbling in the margins to a dedicated drawing practice. Figuring out where to begin and what to draw can be challenging. But you have to start drawing somewhere, and you can start where you are, with this book in your hand.

In this book you will find step-by-step illustrations to help you draw. There are no written instructions as all the illustrations are self-explanatory. Just follow the steps and you will be able to draw any car in this book. Also use the following pro-tip if you have trouble drawing anything. You can take the help of art grids if you find it difficult to draw proportionately. Anytime you want to draw something that requires accuracy (a portrait, a pet, a vehicle, a complex still life), you might want to use the grid method. It allows you to break the reference down into smaller and more manageable segments. Even the best artists in the world will struggle to draw complex objects purely by eye, without any visual aid like construction lines.

There's no avoiding it: learning to draw well takes practice. Don't worry about any mistakes you make along the way. Every single bit of effort counts. There is no such thing as wasted effort in drawing. So just..

"Practice, practice, practice, and don't give up."